INCOMING

VETERAN WRITERS ON
RETURNING HOME

EDITED BY

JUSTIN HUDNALL
JULIA DIXON EVANS
ROLF YNGVE

SO SAY WE ALL

Book design by Adam Vieyra

ISBN: 978-0-9883686-8-2

So Say We All (SSWA) is a San Diego-based 501c3
non-profit organization that provides arts education
to populations without access, and supports local
artists through showcase opportunities and
peer-to-peer counseling.

www.sosayweallonline.com

ACKNOWLEDGEMENTS

This work would not have been possible without the support of the San Diego and Oceanside Public Libraries, among whose officers Marc Chery, Erwin Magbanua, Jennelise Yolanda, and Kara West deserve particular credit for their tireless commitment to serving their communities in new and inventive ways.

We are enormously grateful to Cal Humanities for their support and inclusion of our programming in their "War Comes Home" initiative, which inspired and continues to inspire a dialogue whose end result is nothing short of life-saving. They are good people who do good work, Felicia Kelley and Angelica Dongollo especially.

Special thanks to Ron Capps and the Veterans Writing Project, as well as the good people at Poets and Writers, for being magnificent advocates and force multipliers when we put our call out to veteran writers for their stories. We wouldn't have made nearly so many great friends without them.

We dedicate this collection of stories about returning home from war to the men and women who never came home.

TABLE OF CONTENTS

INTRODUCTION

So Say We All was incorporated as a nonprofit in 2009 with a mission to help people, all people, tell their stories and tell them better. The organization does not distinguish between people who identify as writers, and those who just have an amazing story and the drive to share it, because we believe storytelling is the one art form every human participates in, has to for the sake of their mental health. We offer services in education, performance, and publishing to the public at large, and also to groups we feel have been talked about more than heard from.

Veterans are one such group we believe has been disproportionately the topic of conversation rather than of an invited participant, and we feel that's a special kind of injustice. So Say We All is based in San Diego, where the military is so entrenched that when the movie Top Gun debuted, it was received as a documentary; speaking as a child of the 80's, the exaggeration is slight.

Veterans and active duty military are part of our life here in Southern California. We have the SEALS, the Marines, the Navy, Army, flyboys, spouses and children, nurses, doctors, and to our great shame, the homeless and deported who once wore the uniform. They are our friends, our lovers, our children, and parents. They are us.

That isn't the case everywhere in America, and without knowing them as individuals, it's dangerously easy to treat the idea of veterans as a bloc, one that just can't seem to get its act together once it comes back from deployment. The discussion about veteran suicide, Post-Traumatic Stress, the propensity for self-medication and addiction and domestic violence, is all too often tinged with a passive judgement, as though it were an unfortunate virus that affected a small minority whom civilians aren't really accountable to.

There is no way to come home from a momentous journey unchanged, without facing the struggle of reassimilation into a home that can never be the same as it was remembered. The mythology of our species shows us that has been the case across all cultures for all time. It does not matter if that journey involved combat, killing, or the fear of being killed. It is always a lonely path, shared only by a brother and sisterhood of fellow travelers that necessity demands are separated from one another upon their return, back into the fold of well-meaning strangers, who, in the vast majority, cannot relate to what the veteran has been through.

So what we set out to do was ask those who took that journey: What was it like to return? We gave one line of guidance in our prompt, that the writers could speak to any subject matter they wanted, but were not obligated to anything. The result, this book, contains responses from active duty and veterans alike, men and women, gay and straight, across the multitude of ethnicity. In total: our military as it serves, free of politics, free of censure, a citizen army.

We hope this collection helps bridge the inevitable and blameless gulf of understanding that comes from asking so few to carry so large a burden as our national defense. We hope you enjoy it as a piece of art also. More than anything, we're honored to be able to steward these stories, and grateful to the men and women who trusted us to do so.

Executive Director, So Say We All
Justin Hudnall,
San Diego, 2015

HOME INVASION

By Benjamin Busch

n the spring of 2001 we were rehearsing for wars we no longer expected to happen. Everything we carried was green and we weren't thinking of deserts yet. We stayed on our bases and made believe, attacking ourselves and then going home, over and over. We drove to drills from suburbs through the back roads of Virginia, paved colonial routes that wound through the countryside. Old farms had been bought by the government to be used as military training ranges, and though the settlements had been removed from maps long ago, a building would sometimes appear adrift in the wilderness. While Marines hunted each other dressed as woodland, I found a farmhouse deep in the trees. It was long forsaken, the road to it filled with oaks, all of the children born there gone. The toil to clear this land had been consumed by the soil; no lines had been left by generations trudging behind teams of horses to cut furrows in the orange clay. No plow here now, and no sword. But the home stood, its thin tin roof splitting rain over the empty rooms. A farmhouse was as much a fortress as could be built by a family. Seeing one so completely surrendered was a quiet loss of tremendous magnitude. Its open windows, hollow interior and century of stories drew me inside.

The door had been torn away, its rusted hinges still in place, and I stepped in to find a single room. There was a small addition on the right where a kitchen had been, but the stove had been carried off and the floor had fallen in. I went up the tilted stairs as if they were made of loose plates of glass. The second story was bleak, its bare plaster peeling from the lath. The roof had leaked and the floorboards at the top of the stairs were soft with rot. I stayed close to the wall and crept around the damp spot as if it were already a hole. It was like walking on a ledge. There was a small access door to the attic space above the kitchen. It was nailed shut. If an undiscovered relic remained, it would be in there. A mason jar of coins, a photograph, a child's toy, anything. I pried it open with my Leatherman tool and cool air poured out as if I had broken the seal on a tomb. It took a while to inch my shoulders past the nails in the frame and then slide half way into the cavity. My belt caught and my eyes adjusted.

A dark shape loomed in a corner, very close, and it seemed to swell in size. It let out a shocking croak and spilled a vile burst of vomit toward me. The odor was stunning, a putrid soup of carrion, and I struggled to back out, stuck half way through the tiny door, one arm in, one arm out, the vulture hopping awkwardly away toward a gash in the roof, the tip of its wing swiping my face as it passed. The stench was overpowering and I became careless with desperation to escape, finally ripping myself out of the wall and stumbling backward as if I'd been shot. I stood, gasping curses, in the center of the rotten floor I had so carefully avoided on my way in. The boards burst and I fell, my arms stopping me for an instant, but the spongy wood gave way and my weight pulled me through. I landed with a thud that seemed to shake the house, moist plaster pouring onto me with fragments of floor and mouse droppings. I rose slowly, surprised to find myself uninjured, the last man standing, my arms stretched out like I was balancing on a beam. I waited for the walls to fold in on me, but after a wary pause I crept outside as if even the sound of my steps might shatter the room. I looked back at the house, the gutted dwelling of the vulture. Seeing this place in its final indignity, I wondered who had been the last one to walk out, close the door, and know that no one would ever return.

The house had suffered the terrible moment when no one lived to call it their home. A leak formed in the roof, started as no more than a tear in the sheets of tin, the rain creeping in and beginning to tap on the floor of a bedroom, insects and fungus following the dark path of the water and rotting through the rooms below. Over time its shape changed, roof sagging, windows squeezed until the brittle glass split into shards and dropped into the drip line. The rooms shifted, plaster breaking off and littering the sinking floors. It would stand impossibly like this for a while, then suddenly splinter into the grave of its cellar. It was like a stranded ship that took fifty years to sink. The chimney may stand for several more decades, finally weakened by its solitude, the freeze and thaw lifting its rocks apart, heaping them around the ashen hearth like a burial mound.

I circled it one last time and found the rim of a wagon wheel, some broken cork-top bottles and the single arm of a porcelain doll. It was only three inches long, stained by rusted cans and soil, but it was complete, its five fingers cupped and fused. I wrapped it in a glove and headed back into the war games. Days later, in my own home, I placed the pale arm in a drawer that held worn sea shells picked from beaches. They looked like pieces of the same body, a tiny child blown apart.

By spring of 2005 I was in Ramadi, Iraq on my second combat tour. The city was made of concrete and metal, all the homes poured or built with hollow blocks. The floors could not rot, but they could be cracked and the city often shook with car bombs or IEDs, smoke rising out of neighborhoods full of children. Some homes had been collapsed by the war, all of the rooms crushed into a thin pile of fragments and rebar. Our enemies fought us from houses and apartments, holding families hostage or driving them out. They brought violence and we responded in kind, keeping the city frightened. Our patrols took sporadic fire and we fought house to house because there was no other choice. We were left to search homes we had searched many times before, the women and children gathered in one room waiting for us to leave, knowing that the men we sought were already gone. They lived in between all of us.

On these streets gunfire sounded like it came from all directions so we reacted as if it had, spreading out into every home around us while mobile units circled the perimeter to catch our assailants if they fled. We hoped that if we moved quickly enough, we might trap them in the second story of a house, their fingers still guilty with gunpowder. On one such day a Marine in my patrol was hit by a sniper and we rushed, passing through a walled courtyard with our eyes on the windows. The front door was unlocked and we pulled it open, leading the way in with our rifles. I stayed at the bottom of the stairs aiming up as Marines went from room to room downstairs. The house was empty but clean, just vacated, already haunted by its family's hurried departure. There was still dry bread on a kitchen counter. A Marine covered me as I went up the stairs followed by another, both of us watching the doorway at the top, our eyes tight to our rifle sights. Our concentration shrank the space, closed the stairway in, and our steps echoed as if we were mechanical and composed of something harder than flesh. I made entry into the room and was surprised by my own reflection in a mirror. My finger involuntarily tightened on my trigger as I saw what I would look like to anyone else. I had never seen myself this way. I swept the room, stopping on a plastic doll's head, its blue fractured eyes looking back at me. The eyes were the color and the head the size of the baby girl I had left at home, my daughter, born just months before I deployed. An Iraqi child had worn much of the hair off the doll with affection, then suddenly left it behind, perhaps one possession too many to carry. The room was empty, a few brass shell casings on the floor, wardrobes left open, the house quickly abandoned by a family escaping with nowhere to go but somewhere else in the war. I was the danger as much as anyone else. I took a photograph of the doll and went back out to the street.

I patrolled past the house for months afterward, entering to clear it again from time to time after the sound of gunfire. The doll's head remained in the child's empty room, the last of the family that never returned. By the end of the year I was gone too. When I arrived home, I looked at my house, door locked, glass in its windows, its rooms filled with our lives and our history in objects, the porcelain arm still in a drawer. But the monument of home had changed, its impermanence now imaginable, our disappearance inevitable, forests and invasion no longer as distant as I had believed. I wonder who will find our ruins and why the last of us will have left it to fall. I wonder where the war will move.

HOW TO FEEL ASHAMED
FOR THINGS YOU NEVER DID
By Matthew Young

W hen I return from my first deployment, my family is waiting at Camp San Mateo. Our company rolls in on charter buses from March Air Force Base in the evening. We exit the buses to a parade deck full of screaming families. Some of my salts who got out before or during the deployment are outside the armory throwing beers over the fence as we turn in rifles and heavy weapon systems.

The camp guard gives up.

I find my family wandering the basketball court at the center of the barracks calling my name. Not everyone, but most of them: grandparents, aunt, fiancée. I want so badly to be happy when I see them.

My family has rooms at a hotel in San Clemente, California, just outside Pendleton. I have leave for ninety-six hours. Four days. The thought of four days with them quickens my heart. In the car I place my sweaty palm to the smooth, cool flesh of my fiancée's thigh, and the muscle beneath her skin tightens for a lightning strike of seconds. From the front seat, my grandfather talks about the drive from Mount Shasta to Camp Pendleton. He talks about the Grapevine and great distances and how no one else knows how to make his mochas the way he likes them aside from the chippie at the coffee hut back home. I listen, stare at the city lights, and marvel at the lack of tangled wires, at the people walking around after ten at night, at the smiles, at the clean roads.

In the hotel room I drink beer and liquor and smoke cigarettes. I am quiet at first. Going from Iraq to Kuwait to California in less than a week is shocking to my system, is throwing my neurons out of whack. I've had a drink or two in the last eight months, only a swig of whisky here or there. This is something else altogether.

Because of the drink I'm tossing down my gullet, later on I won't remember how I begin talking about the deployment. But I do.

I have not lied to them, yet. I tell them what I think are funny stories about Keene shitting himself and trying to talk after our truck was blown sky high by a culvert bomb, about Charlie falling down a dune during lieutenant-mandated forced trash pick up while taking sniper fire, about detaining a twelve-year-old boy, about being ambushed in the back of a Humvee and laughing.

During these stories, my family filters from the room, excusing themselves to sleep until it's only me, my aunt, and my fiancée. The silences between us make me nervous. The silences feel like expectation. My drunk mind's interpretation of perceived expectation covers the women's faces like a sheen of sweat.

What I haven't realized in that moment, what I'll come to understand later, is that they're not expecting anything, but are instead pleading, begging, and screaming for me to shut up. If I could erase the drunk from my brain I'd notice the facial torsion, widened eyes, crimped mouths. But instead, the warped faces begin to look to me like confused faces, questioning, wondering where the real story is. Like they are waiting for an answer as to why I am the way I have become, and all the talk I've vomited on them hasn't been enough.

So now I tell a lie. I tell them about a made up village and a fantasy house within the village and imagined insurgents within the fantasy house and fictional grenades and bullets I used to kill those invented insurgents defending the fantasy house. I try to think of realistic films, secondhand stories from my salts, books I've read, anything to tell convincing details of bullet holes and blood spatter and viscera. This feels, to me, like an explanation of the individual phenomena of experience, this black and white infallible story of good versus evil. A story where I don't feel as though I have to explain my actions. A story where I get to feel, for once, like a hero.

In the morning, my head aches and alcohol sweat coats my skin like wax. There's a tough, meaty, sick feeling in the ethereal place beyond my stomach, between soul and body, floating around inside of me--a shattered figurative pelvic bone where I birthed my lie into the world. When I attempt to remember the previous night my pulse quickens, my head grows light and my palms clam as they did the previous evening against the smooth clean flesh of my fiancée's leg.

In the car on the way to breakfast no one makes eye contact with me. Or maybe, I cannot bring myself to make eye contact with them. Or maybe I'm imagining all that. I wonder what I said, verbatim. I wonder if I made up anything other than my perfect story. Maybe I did. Maybe I didn't. I think maybe I should ask what I talked about. I wonder if my family would recount the story I told. Will they remember? Maybe they'll forget about it, I think. They probably don't remember, I think. I should tell the truth and apologize, I think. I'll just say, 'Sorry for last night,' I think. I think, They'll understand, they are my family, of course they will understand.

I open my mouth to speak.

My grandfather pulls out of the hotel parking lot in the path of a passenger bus and I have a very real, not fictitious anxiety attack. Trash on the roadside puckers me, a woman in a hijab sheaths my fingernails into my palms. I think my aunt must notice my reactions because she eyeballs me and tries to make a joke about my grandfather's driving. I cannot manage a laugh.

We are at a restaurant, we eat, and begin to talk again. But now I think maybe we had never stopped talking in the first place. I enjoy the huevos rancheros and let sticky brine into my nostrils and take my first full breath in eight months.

So the lie becomes a scratch on the roof of my mouth I can't stop tonguing. Passively nagging and pulling but always there. Later, I'll tell the lie to friends, to acquaintances, to other marines. After a time, I'm ashamed to not tell the lie. After a while that thick sick feeling, the thing beyond my guts floating in the ether, becomes a dull throb, a bit of pressure next to the spine or behind the eyes or inside the ribcage, but doesn't disappear. It won't ever disappear.

QUEEN'S CREEK

By Brandon Lingle

Midway into a late-night run, I veer down the narrow trail to my neighborhood's dock. It is November 2011, and I've been home from Iraq for barely a week. The oyster-shell path glows under porch light shards as it curves away from the homes and plunges into a swath of forest. I navigate the wooden stairs that zigzag down the hillside. At the bottom, a pier spans a hundred yards over marshland into the main channel of Queen's Creek.

Surrounded by bases from every service, the stream runs through the epicenter of America's military might, past and present—a nexus of American violence. Just a few miles from the ruins of Jamestown and the monument marking Washington and Rochambeau's victory at Yorktown, this ribbon of brackish water reinforced key defensive lines for colonists, revolutionaries, rebels, and spies. The creek anchored a palisade shielding English colonists from the Powhatans. During the Civil War, Magruder and Longstreet used it to bolster Confederate lines against McClellan's Army of the Potomac.

The mouth of this York River tributary forms the western edge of land DuPont used as a dynamite plant during the Great War. Workers lived in a company town named after Russell Penniman, the creator of ammonia-based dynamite. A government report says the factory produced 54,000 shells daily, and thousands of tons of explosives were unaccounted for when the plant closed shortly after World War I. The site became the Navy's Cheatham Annex during World War II. Today, the base remains a Navy storage facility and recreation area, and is an E.P.A. Superfund site thanks to decades of toxic and medical waste dumping. Just beyond Cheatham lies Yorktown Naval Weapons Center, current home to most of the Navy's explosives.

Queen's Creek also serves as the eastern boundary of a government training site called Camp Peary, which was carved from land annexed in 1942 that included the towns of Magruder and Bigler's Mill. Originally a Navy base, where 150,000 Seabees trained for World War II duty, today the site is officially titled the Armed Forces Experimental Training Activity, but most call it The Farm. The consensus is that the CIA uses the base to train recruits. I see bearded Camp Peary guys during my 7 a.m. gas station coffee stop—lots of Velcro and pockets, tattoos, and grey t-shirts with a crossbow logo on the chest. Blacked-out choppers buzz my house every few weeks, and I wonder if geared-up operators hang in the open doors, eyeballing my neighborhood through the green and black of night vision goggles. Sometimes, when I barbeque or toss the ball to my kids, I hear machine gun fire from across the creek. Every couple of months, around 3 a.m., Camp Peary explosions pummel my home. Shockwaves rattle walls, picture frames, and my children's nerves. The bombs jolt me awake, and I feel the same adrenaline-tinged heartbeat that I felt after the explosions in Baghdad. People aren't disintegrating at Camp Peary, but the blasts share the same ominous aftermath as many war-zone booms: silence. Most times you never know the explosions' cause or consequence.

Across the water from Camp Peary's black ops and barbed wire, the creek flows into a bastion of recreation. Docks, clubhouses, pools, and mansions now guard the sloping banks. At New Quarter Park the trails ease past the remnants of Confederate earthworks. Sometimes I hear of nearby residents digging up cannonballs, musket rounds, or arrowheads in their vegetable gardens.

* * *

Camp Peary's choppers are silent this night, but my footsteps rattle the dock's faded planks above the drone of vehicles blasting across the I-64 bridge, slung low across the creek two hundred yards downstream. The dock's two-by-fours reflect a bony light under the blood moon. I hear a splash in the slough off to my right, and I keep my pace despite a tweak in my chest. The tidal stream resembles crude, flowing thick, slow, and silent toward the York, Chesapeake, and the Atlantic beyond. As I near the end of the dock I spot a person silhouetted against the dim sky. Five meters out I apologize for disturbing his peace.

He says, "No worries."

He leans into the rail flanking a line of empty beer bottles. He pinches a wad of tobacco into his lower lip. I breathe a whiff of minty leaves and crave a chew, but remember that I quit when I left Iraq. I'm still breathing hard and sweating as we navigate through intros and the weather. I learn his name is Will and that he's on leave, en route from a Fort Sill artillery job to Special Forces School at Fort Bragg. I mention I'm on leave too. Two weeks off before getting back to work at Langley Air Force Base. In the darkness, I discern the outline of his parted hair and collared shirt. The hazy sky, commingled with swamp stench and car exhaust, yanks my mind back to Baghdad. On a certain level I savor the smell of the primordial mud riding the November breeze as our discussion slides toward Mesopotamia. He completed his second Iraq tour a few weeks before I returned from my first, during the death throes of the nine-year odyssey.

"This tour was a joke compared to the first," he says. "Last time we could shoot back."

I nod in the dark.

In the past, American forces would fire back on the spots

where insurgents launched rockets or mortars toward our bases. More often than not, the bad guys didn't stick around to watch. Cobbled launchers of scrap iron, batteries, and washing machine timers lobbed their weapons automatically. The U.S. barrage that followed could sometimes kill innocents and destroy their neighborhoods. As Operation Iraqi Freedom shifted toward New Dawn, and Americans left Iraqi cities, the policy shifted too, and we stopped shooting back.

"It doesn't add up," he says. "What good is an artillery unit that can't fire back?"

I begin to think that it's a good thing his unit wasn't pummeling neighboring Iraqis, and then I'm ambushed by the reality: it's much easier to think that way when you're safe at home on a brisk autumn night.

"Makes about as much sense as carrying unloaded weapons in a war zone," I say. "Some soldiers didn't even have their own ammo. The bosses were more afraid of our own guys. Accidental discharge."

"Or, how about bases not having overhead cover?"

Overhead cover—expensive armor usually built over soldiers' quarters and dining facilities—can help minimize the damage from insurgent rockets and mortars. Even after years of conflict, most military Forward Operating Bases in Iraq had very little overhead cover, but virtually all State Department people lived in up-armored facilities. Leaders explained that Department of Defense bases in Iraq would close at the end of the year and State Department sites would remain open, justifying the expense, but for the military people on the ground, this translates roughly into: "You are expendable."

Fifteen service members died in June '11, the deadliest month for Americans in Iraq since the height of the surge in '08. The worst attack came when a Shiite militia attacked a Baghdad FOB with improvised rockets. It's tough to say whether or not overhead cover might have helped save the six soldiers roused from their bunks as their world closed in just before dawn that June 6th.

"We pay millions to build up the Iraqi military, but aren't

willing to spend the extra cash to protect our troops?"

"The Iraqis I worked with could barely fix a flat on their Humvee," he says. "I'm not sure what we achieved in the last year."

"We talked, drank tea, and got lots of people hurt and killed." Some worked to keep the war going, riding around the country on helicopters and selling weapons to Iraqis.

"Can we keep 50,000 troops in Iraq, please? 25,000? 10,000? 5,000? How about 150?" A pause. "I killed a sixteen-year-old boy," he says. "Our battalion's only kill this deployment."

I stare at his shadow on the dock, and I feel a stab of fall air through my damp t-shirt.

"Outside Kirkuk. Got pinned down by someone taking pot shots," he says. "We figured out where the shooter was, and the lieutenant colonel froze. He was nearly crying. Lying on the ground. Ordered me to take the shooter out. So, I did. Just a barefoot kid with a rusty AK. He fell in a drainage ditch. I remember the muddy water flowing over his feet."

Like the vast majority of service members, I've never fired a weapon in combat let alone killed anyone. I think about how I'd have reacted.

"Damn dude," I say. "I'm not sure what to say."

"It's okay," he says. "Maybe I accomplished something while I was over there."

We talk for more than an hour. I learn that his dad is a Vietnam vet who teaches combat skills at Camp Peary. In addition to extreme daily workouts, Will plans to run land navigation courses through the local woods during his week of leave, in preparation for the years of special operations training to come. The prospect of endless days of mental, physical, and emotional trials excites him.

He hopes to eventually deploy to Afghanistan, or maybe Iraq again. While most American forces are set to leave in December 2011, a military presence providing security cooperation as part of ongoing State Department efforts will continue in Iraq for years.

"I'll handle whatever they throw at me," he says. "I'm up to the challenge."

With that, he lobs his empty beer bottle in a mortar arc toward the water. The glass catches hints of moonlight before shattering the creek's surface in a watery blast. Concentric ripples run silently from the epicenter out into the darkness, just as military forces and government operatives flow out and into the world from this place that I call home. And, just as tide runs in to fill the creek, so too do the unending consequences of our military odysseys.

I wish him luck, shake his hand, and turn away. As I walk toward shore, my mind drifts back before my deployment, to when my family and I watched summer sunsets, walking the dock. When we first arrived in tidewater Virginia we complained to each other about the sewer smell permeating our neighborhood. Eventually I realized this was normal for our intertidal stream, the natural byproduct of growth and decay churning in the water and the mud. I'd point out raccoon tracks lining the mire or snapping turtles holding fast in small water pockets. At the end of the dock we tossed lines with hooked minnows we'd scooped from their schools in a mesh bucket trap. We'd hope to catch croaker but usually pulled blue crabs.

Time after time I'd hoist the crabs onto the deck and my seven-year-old twin boys would taunt the crustaceans with sticks. The creatures always retreated with their claws up, like miniature boxers blocking incoming blows, or shielding their eyes from the sun. My boys jumped and laughed until the crabs found their way to the edge and fell sprawling backward, back into their brown water murk.

"Queen's Creek" was originally published in Guernica and selected as a notable in Best American Essays 2013

THE PRICE OF A KINDNESS
By G. Michael Smith

"I got the cell phone. Matt's already on the line," Sylvia said, holding it out to me.

"Hey, Matt. It's a German Shepherd – looks pretty well cared for. What do you want me to do?"

"See if you can find an entry wound."

"I already checked, and I can't see anything."

"Okay, can you move him?"

"Well, he was pretty terrified when I got here, but I got him gentled down some... Let me see."

I pushed gently on his shoulder, and the dog rolled onto his side. As he did, the loose skin on his chest moved up, and I saw it. It was just a small hole in the beautiful brown-and-black coat of a dog with the long nose and proud ears of his breed.

"Found it, Matt. Entry wound on his lower chest; looks like a .22 round."

"Okay, good. Check for bleeding."

I checked.

"Dammit."

"What?"

"The wound isn't sucking, but there's blood on his lips and some coming out his nose."

"Okay, Mike. You can bring him in if you want, but all I can do is put him out of his misery."

I kept my hand on the dog's neck, stroking. When I pulled it away, he looked up at me and whimpered. I put my hand on him again.

"Matt, all that'll do is put him through another forty-five minutes of hell. I'll do it here,"

"All right. If anybody objects, you can refer them to me. Sorry I couldn't help."

"Okay if I refer them to you if I find the son of a bitch who did this?" It seemed to me the shooter needed killing more than the dog did.

"I can help you out with the dog. Mike, but I have to draw the line at humans."

"Yeah. Even people who kill for the fun of it. Just askin.'"

I said goodbye and handed the phone back to a hovering Sylvia.

"Mike, I'm sorry… I just couldn't do it," she said.

"It's okay."

I talked to the dog and stroked his head and ears some, telling him about chasing balls and chewing on bones. Sylvia walked back toward her car and away from it. I told the beautiful German Shepherd everything would be okay.

I pulled the trigger.

A neighbor driving past stopped and volunteered to take care of burying him. I was already staring at nothing, but I thanked Therrel, and I hoped he knew I was grateful.

The next day, I rested. I sat on my top patio step overlooking the creek, and I rested. I watched the deer come to the creek, saw the leaves on the trees, the green tree line. I watched the slow progression of clouds across the sky, saw a glint of sun from a high-flying jet; the flash of light from their canopies as they rolled into dives, steep and fast. It seemed impossible that they could pull out of it, but they did, and a quarter mile of jungle would go up in napalm flames beneath them. And I looked at the trees.

We could not tell if they were fishermen or soldiers, so for our survival, they were soldiers. All of them. It mattered only that the shot was accurate when you took it, because a board and search can go to Hell in an instant. And I watched the deer drink, and I watched the Blue Heron fish in the creek.

I spent almost a week …resting. After days, the trees on the far side of the creek seemed to become less of a tree line. After days, thoughts of the flat trajectory and heat trail of a 30-06 round faded. Slowly, I began to let go of looking at the hidden spots in the woods and assessing them as ambush sites, all the while staring at nothing.

Yes, there are things I can do that are hard, and even though I learned those things in a hellish place, I realize now there is value in them. I brought wisdom home with me, and when others might not know what to do, I can keep going. I learned to keep my head clear when it matters, knowing that I can delay paying the price until it's over.

The dog hadn't needed to spend more time alive while he slowly drowned in his own blood, and I had known the amount I'd pay before I pulled the trigger. I paid it for his sake, and it was okay, because I live on twenty acres, where I can sit on my patio overlooking the creek and woods. It's beautiful here, restful and quiet.

HALF ASLEEP IN THE BLUE LIGHT LOUNGE
by Kurt Kalbfleisch

I t is always late-evening dark in here, but I've got friends sitting
to the left and right of me, and there's music. "Friends" might
be the wrong word. They're people I trust. Really trust, like I
know they would walk through fire for me. I know because
we've practiced it. Walking through fire for each other. With actual fire. If a guy will put on six layers of clothes and go stand in
a 500 degree room for you, you can trust him.

I call these men "brother" even though they're not my family,
except they are my family, just not the kind of family where I
know their wives' names or how old their kids are.

The music we listen to isn't what I'd set up a channel on Pandora for. It's really just information being passed on the radio
with an occasional crypto screech, like something from a Philip
Glass concerto, which I definitely don't want to create a Pandora
channel for. Still, it's music: satellite data jazz, man.

Chief LaPlume called it "The Blue Light Lounge," and we
all slump in front of our consoles, gazing into orange screens,
getting wasted on radar scope dope, waiting. Recruiters won't tell
you about the waiting. We wait for everything. I mostly wait for
my relief. I trust my relief with my life, but I don't trust him to
wake up on time, so I keep an eye on the clock, every damn day.

When there's a gap in the music, the conversation flows. OS2 Greenup likes orchestrating lists of things like all the slang terms we can think of for vagina. Our list of terms for penis took days to finish and ended up being a hundred and fifty items long. Because my brothers are, like, twelve.

So it's not unusual when the watch officer suddenly screams, "Jesus Christ, Heine, put your clothes on!" Greenup had suggested that OS2 Heine didn't have the balls to stand the rest of his watch naked. One does not decline a challenge in the Blue Light Lounge.

Sometimes, there's mail. Actual mail, which I'd call snail mail if snails could swim. When it gets quiet, which is rare, you'll find one or two of the guys reading a letter.

On this particular night, I have mail from home. The date on the postmark is from three weeks ago. E-mail is not a thing yet. It's thick, though, and that's exciting: lots of news from home.

Not really. There is a two page letter, front and back of one page, so really a page and a half. And there is a bundle of pages from Consumer Reports. A small part of me knows that she didn't mean to annoy me, but the rest of me? The rest of me is annoyed.

Her letter begins with a complaint that I have not been holding up my end of the conversation, as if one can have a conversation with six weeks between responses. She hasn't been receiving enough letters from me, though she doesn't tell me how many letters she wants. I feel defensive and guilty. I haven't written as often as I would like, but my silence has been justified. For most of January, no mail was permitted on or off the ship. Operational security, we're told.

It makes sense. We had just launched ten Tomahawk missiles into Iraq, destroying Saddam Hussein's nuclear weapons program.

I wrote eleven pages about it, determined to make up for what I knew had been an uncomfortable silence. I wrote in detail about how it felt to do the job we'd trained for. I wrote about the adrenaline rush, the dead-serious moments, the quiet, the roar of missile boosters, the scramble to launch an extra missile when a Tomahawk from another ship exploded over their heads, the raucous celebration by shipmates who had merely stood by and watched, the football game on television with nachos and near-beer on the mess decks, the half-time interruption when the White House Press Secretary announced what we'd done. I wrote about getting the horrifying news that a missile had fallen into a hotel lobby. About not knowing if it was our missile. About not knowing if it was my missile. Eleven pages.

I tick the weeks off on my fingers. Our letters must have passed each other in the mail. I feel better, though later, months later, I will not.

Most of the rest of her letter is a treatise on why I should abandon my plan to buy a new car when I get home. It is a plan we had agreed to when I let her talk me into selling my truck before deployment. I decide not to mention it when I write back, because it'll be six weeks before I can read her response, and by then, we'll be almost home. The pages from Consumer Reports are, to her, the final word on the subject. There is no use in arguing.

The last paragraph of her letter stops my heart. She tells me she spent a wonderful weekend in Mexico, riding horses on the beach. With a friend.

She means a male friend. Suspicion ripples my thoughts, making it feel as though I'm viewing the world from under water, except that I can breathe.

I don't respond to the letter from home. I can't think of anything to say.

We pass through the Strait of Hormuz and head for home. The ship lurches through heavy seas and except for the poor bastard who has never managed to get his sea legs, we're happy. The Blue Light Lounge smells like strong coffee and weak vomit, so maybe not entirely happy. Relieved. Relieved is a much better word.

We're home and we are six weeks from home.

In Hong Kong, I search for a payphone. The very idea of the coming conversation makes me uneasy. Against all hope, the call goes through. I ask about Mexico. She tells me it's nothing. I ask her directly: Are you sleeping with him? She laughs and puts our daughter on the phone. Heidi is four, and the sound of her voice makes me giddy. And then she talks mostly about the new man in her life. The new man in her mother's life. I feel dizzy and nauseous.

Three weeks from home.

There isn't much for me to do on watch in the Blue Light Lounge, so I mostly sit with my hands in my coat pockets, collar turned up against the chill of the air conditioning, and think about my new car. If my brothers notice me brooding, they don't say anything. I want to hate them, at least a little. They are my home and I have to leave them soon, and it will hurt too much if I love them when I go. I convince myself that they are the reason my marriage is ending. The reason my marriage has ended. The home I'm returning to doesn't exist anymore. I need a new home. A 1993 Ford Probe GT. Steel blue. My wife and I will stop at the Mile of Cars on our way home the day I arrive. I know to the dollar what I will spend. I know because of Consumer Reports.

Two weeks from home.

We stop in Pearl Harbor, to pick up fathers and sons, brothers and nephews, guests who will ride the ship home with us. My father is among them. He knows something's wrong, but I don't tell him, can't tell him, have no idea what words to use to tell him that his son is a failure and cannot love.

Nine days from home.

At sea, there are air shows and flybys and great thumping walls of water. There are guests who want tours, sea stories, gunnery demonstrations, steel beach picnics and burgers and water balloons. And nine last days and nights at home in the Blue Light Lounge.

In the Blue Light Lounge, my father sits next to me and we talk about everything but that my marriage is failing, has already failed weeks ago, and I am still twenty-four hours from beginning the two years it will take for me to learn I could have done nothing to stop it.

The music in the Blue Light Lounge is buoyant. My brothers are laughing with their sons and their fathers, a warm cacophony. I sit beside my father with my hands in my coat pockets, still not talking about that first view of her in the crowd on the pier, not talking about that first embrace. Talking about my new car. We talk about philosophy, about duty and honor and time away from home. I am at home and eight hours from home. I transfer in a week, and though I don't want to leave, I have to and so I just want to get it over with. I have to leave home to go home.

The crowd is on the pier, of course, and they are joyfully noisy. She is not among them, not at first. Later, she will admit that she could not bring herself to leave her lover's bed; but right now, I can only wonder, even though I know. I know. I have known for weeks.

The crowds are still there, at least, when she arrives, gloriously, colorfully late. She greets me with a smile and a hug and later, I'll see that it looked pretty convincing on camera. We go home, my wife, our daughter, my father, and me. We do not stop at the Mile of Cars. My father arranges for my wife and me to have a few hours alone. She pours shots of tequila. It is not a celebration.

Afterwards, I feel like a chore. I know that I will fail to be what she wants, just as I always have. She insists that I buy a used Honda Civic, instead of the new Probe she agreed to seven months ago. So I did.

Two weeks later, in her brother's kitchen, her family asked about the Tomahawk strike they saw on CNN in January. "Was it you?"

"Yes," I reply. "Didn't Kim tell you?"

All eyes turn to her.

"I don't know what you do," she says.

"What about my letter?"

She shrugs, dismisses it and me with a wave of her hand.

Less than a week later, on my way home from work, I say, "Fuck it," out loud, and stop at the Mile of Cars to buy that goddamned Ford Probe GT. It is steel blue and it reminds me of my home in the Blue Light Lounge. I traded in the Civic, deliberately accepting less for it than she wanted. I pissed her off, but I wanted to. She demanded to know why I bought the car and I told her that I wanted it because of Consumer Reports.

On the day she drove away with our children, I opened a filing cabinet and found a letter. It is unopened, but I know it is eleven pages long.

HOMECOMING

by Robert Shaw

I flew home with a different unit because that was the way it worked. I had sweated, bled, and lived with my friends and brothers for over a year, and now I rode back with soldiers I didn't know.

To me Kuwait was like some large international bus station. To many back home it may sound exotic and dangerous, but to someone who had been, "outside the wire," the Burger King and civilian clothes showed Kuwait's true colors. No war here, no building the team through shared pain and suffering. Only sitting and waiting for something else, either to come or go. It was the wartime equivalent of a fat girl who signs up for cheerleading so she can sound attractive. Kuwait was not a war, it was where you caught your transfer either to or from war. I sat there waiting for a bus to the US for three days.

When I landed there was no parade, no big event, just a gym with strangers' families in it. I added my weapon to a massive heap and said goodbye to the thing I'd held so closely. The stranger formation marched into the gym in a mild homecoming show. I snuck in the back door and looked for my wife. I saw her. She looked different, had gotten braces. She'd been cheating on me.

The house was very clean and quiet. Like a museum to a life

I had all but forgotten. It reminded me of those movies where parents lose a child and keep their room perfectly intact to help memories stick close by. This house was like mine but minus me.

None of my clothes fit me anymore so on the second day my wife took me to Wal-Mart. I needed toothpaste, things to wear, and all the other possessions of life. I owned nothing, or at least nothing I needed or could remember.

I lasted about 15 minutes inside the store. A slow tide of excess, fatness, and colors overtook me slowly at first and then so suddenly I had to leave. I felt embarrassed and frustrated. I didn't call it PTSD, I just blamed all the fat people of Wal-Mart. I hadn't seen a civilian woman or store in so long, my mind couldn't handle it. That night I saw old friends from my unit who had been back for weeks. We sang and drank.

We were driving to a party later the first week and I realized I was scanning the side of the road for dead dogs or other places to hide bombs. It was getting dark out and my heart quickened thinking about driving in "white lights" and not going blackout. I was focused on my solo convoy and my wife was justifying her actions over the past year. So I stopped the car and got out. I started walking in the dark, back down the road I had just cleared. I had no problem rucking and even enjoyed it. I could hear her yelling or crying and I kept going. Somehow we made up hours or days or weeks later. I'm not sure what either of us said or how we came to peace but we must have. We took to fighting our own brand of war, marked by emotional insurgency and intermittent, indirect fire of passive-aggressive mortars.

I didn't feel at home at home now. We fought a lot and I didn't seem to understand life. I even punched a hole in a wall over something trivial. I had no idea what I was going to do, no job after the Army, no kids, no war. I was so lost I didn't even know getting lost was a possibility. Home is supposed to be the place you strive for. You work and dream to survive to see it again to enjoy all of its comforts. But when you can't enjoy the things you should, you enter an especially sad place. No joy can come to you for reasons you don't know.

I wasn't in this state necessarily because "bad things occurred" overseas, although they did. I was sad and lonely because I felt empty. Something was missing. Fun, danger, excitement, purpose, drive, friends, explosions, intrigue, exotic lands. All were gone. I had a great time in Iraq and I missed it. Wake up and mow the lawn? Why? Fuck the lawn.

I never really came home.

BEYOND THE LINES
by Kelli Hewlett

Young and without much direction in life, my parents pushed me to join the army. They couldn't afford higher education for me and my younger sister, and this was the only alternative they could think of to make sure that we were educated. My mother was a US Army sergeant stationed at San Diego State University as part of the ROTC program, before finally retiring. After dealing with a multitude of students, she'd come to learn of a field in the military that gave back: a degree that transferred to the civilian world when most did not.

So I found myself in a room along with a dozen of others, silently sobbing with my right hand raised as I was sworn in, the star spangled flag hanging against the wall in the front. After being stationed at Walter Reed Army Medical Center, right in the heart of Washington, D.C., one thing was for sure: I was going to do the rest of my two years and go back home to San Diego, where the sun shone and cold did not exist. From what I've been told, I actually had a primo duty station at Walter Reed. My mom was stationed in Korea when I was a kid and it seemed like she was gone forever. I wanted to know I could always just come back home. She couldn't.

I became a nurse, working on ward 68, a medical surgical unit that dealt with anything from ears/nose/throat cases to the gut. Every so often I would get "lucky" and have a young soldier that needed to stay overnight for an appendectomy, which was actually refreshing. We could talk about movies that were filmed in color, music from this decade, when the average age of my usual patients was 60 and above.

On September 11th, all that changed. I walked into an elderly man's room with his Metamucil in tow; his television was on and his mouth agape. The towers fell. We went to war. Not too much longer after that our troops started to come home, but not in the fashion recruiters like to showcase. There were no surprise visits from GI mommy or daddy in junior's classroom, no hunky Marines showing up early and unannounced at their spouses job, no. Tattered, scathed, and broken both mentally and physically, that's what we saw.

The unit I worked on transformed. The average age of my patients dropped to the early twenties. There were nights where two nurses from each unit in the hospital would make their way downstairs to a makeshift triage area on the third floor, where a bus full of soldiers would pull up out front. There were some who were able to get off on their own, the rest lay in litters waiting to be carried out and placed onto gurneys, their bloodied bandages last changed long ago. We'd make sure they were stable, then figure out where to put them based on injury type and level of care needed.

Other nights a medevac would arrive on the helipad atop the hospital roof. That usually spelled a serious situation. I met one of those helicopters once. The patient died in the process of getting to the states, twice. They needed him to have a new photo military ID, since he was patrolling without one at the time of injury. His dog tags just weren't enough, so they took his picture in-flight. When it was snapped, he was soulless. The fact that he ended up living was beyond me.

The hospital's old rooms, once used for storage, were converted back into rooms that could bear patients. Soldiers were greeted with smiles and stifled tears, "Welcome to Walter Reed." After some time it became a well-oiled machine. Telephone cards and cash aid on debit cards. Family would arrive soon thereafter. The Red Cross was pretty amazing.

There was joy and pain all at once. I have seen so many reunions: A father met his twin girls, only a few months old, for the very first time there. A 19 year old hugged his parents who were so happy just to have their baby back. One young lady was able to reconnect, to her surprise, with her bomb dog. Considering her own injuries and luck just to be alive after an explosive went off, she could only imagine he hadn't survived. He jumped on her bed and she wept for joy, lips trembling, tears streaming. I was happy for myself too, finally getting to see tears of relief.

Too often I watched soldiers' significant others become as distant as their returning counterpart. I've changed IVs while newly reunited couples fidgeted, reluctant to hold a stump where a hand once wore their wedding band, slow to talk about the future. They said it with their eyes, "how do I live with this?" Be it a lost limb, a disfigured face, an affixed bag to the abdomen that will forever collect stool, the couples shared that look. The adjustment is the worst.

We did our duty to fix up their bodies, but we neglected their minds. I was shocked by the amount of patients who wanted to go back to war. They weren't done yet. Their brothers were still over there and they needed to go back.

Others resented their time spent.

"We trained those motherfuckers," one patient of mine exclaimed, "and now here we are getting shot up with our own shit too!"

It was years of this, days and nights that left me drained and exhausted from not knowing how to deal with their baggage, coupled with my own emotions. But I sure as shit couldn't complain. How could I? So I stuck to the script and stuffed it down.

My favorite perk at Walter Reed was the huge celebrity turnout to support the troops. It was VIP central for quite some time, and men and women in uniform got a kick out of it for the most part. I hugged Stevie Nicks and shook the hand of Mic Foley. I almost spilled pee on Justin Timberlake. John Voigt had his own camera guy and took photos with each soldier room-by-room. Tyra Banks and her long-legged crew were pretty popular with the guys. It was really good to see uplifted spirits, even if it was just temporary.

It was almost standard for the soldiers admitted in the hospital to be on some sort of antidepressant or mood stabilizer, bolstered with a sleep aid, done in cookie cutter fashion. Everyone got the same thing. Granted, some changes were made if it didn't seem to help. There were brief meetings with the psych doctor. The ones who displayed serious symptoms or who reached out were seen more. I don't remember many follow-ups though, not for the masses.

Some soldiers came to Walter Reed and never left. Their only escape would be the eventual day pass, but they would soon return for pain and sleeping pills when their short supply ran out. A few even got a three-day pass. I naturally assumed that if you can leave the hospital grounds and don't need to return for three days, well, you don't need to stay in the hospital anymore, but then I wondered if they even wanted to leave. They were used to the structure, the order. They were use to those walls. Maybe there was nothing left for them without the military. They were screaming for help, but all we gave them were pills.

The intake rate slowed down eventually, a couple of years into the war. Still, they just kept coming, and the cycle remained the same. I felt guilty sometimes that I was stateside, that I'd got off easy because I wasn't on the front lines. There was this older soldier I had taken care of. He was a platoon sergeant, a squad leader. He had valor. He listened as I told him how I felt one night, and when I was finished, he told me that I was on the front lines. That his soldiers needed me here to take care of them when they came back.

He'll never know how badly I needed his permission to believe it myself.

COMING HOME
by Sierra Crane

No, it didn't start right away. For the first couple weeks I was home, I was just happy. I couldn't stop smiling. My sister and I were attached at the hip. Everywhere we went, we went together and all I could think about was how amazing it was to be home. Finally home. It was, after all, the first time I'd been able to relax in over two years, so why shouldn't I have been happy?

I had enlisted in the Army National Guard in July of '03, on my 17th birthday, so excited and so proud to be serving my country and doing great things to help the American people. I went to basic training a year later. As soon as I stepped off the plane and into the hot, humid air of South Carolina I feared I'd made the biggest mistake of my life. But I figured that was how everyone felt their first day of BCT. That's what I'd been told. That's what everyone else seemed to think. So I tried to brush it off, tried to focus on my training, instead of the giant hole in my chest from missing my family so much.

It didn't get easier after graduation. At Advanced Infantry Training, the rumors started. My unit was getting deployed, or they weren't. Iraq, Afghanistan, staying home, nobody really knew the answer. Finally I called my NCO, two weeks before my graduation and asked him. "Yes, they're going," he told me. "You're going."

Less than three months later, March, 2005, I left home and began my deployment. To say it was all bad would be a bold-faced lie, to even imply that I had it anywhere near as hard as some veterans would be an insult to them and the sacrifices that they made. So many times I've wondered how I could feel the way I did. What right did I have, when I came home without losing a limb, or a family member, or something obviously life-changing?

I'd been home for two or three weeks when I first realized I wasn't the same—I heard my ex-boyfriend call my mom a bitch and I turned around and punched him.

Would I do it again? Probably. But I never would have before. I was so angry, all the time, and it didn't matter if it was a big problem, or a little one. Something as simple as going to plug in my laptop, and finding a neatly folded pile of clothes in the way. What kind of person would take those clothes and hurl them across the room?

I was that kind of person.

I would walk through the room and my mom and my sister would brace themselves, waiting to see if something else would set me off. Something so tiny, they wouldn't even realize it was there until I was yelling and storming out of the room. They didn't know what was wrong (neither did I), so they didn't know it wasn't their fault.

I would cry alone at night, wanting so badly to be happy, not understanding why I wasn't. I loved my family more than ever because I finally understood what it was like not to have them by my side. But no matter how hard I tried, I couldn't be normal. I couldn't drive down the street and not worry when I saw the cardboard box on the side of the road. I couldn't watch a movie on the 4th of July and not want to curl up in a ball when fireworks went off outside. Eventually, I just wished I could go back. I would've given anything to be given a new set of orders, sending me back to Iraq. Life was simple there. Someone shoots at you, you shoot back. A mortar comes in, you brace yourself. You view everyone as the enemy, just in case.

I'd been home for six months when I finally came to terms with it all. I don't remember exactly what happened, but I'd been upstairs with my sister and I said something awful to her. I knew she was angry and confused. I was never very good at apologies. I just went to bed when she did. I didn't sleep. Soon I was downstairs, pacing back and forth, trying to stifle the sobs so no one would hear me.

Of course, my mom did.

She came downstairs. I fell to the floor and we just sat there. I was crying so hard I couldn't breathe, and to this day I don't know why. I don't know why Iraq changed me so much. I don't know why I was so angry. That certainly isn't the typical reaction you think of when you hear the term PTSD. You also probably don't think of a 19-year-old girl sitting in the turret with a .50 cal in front of her, then, a year later, crying in her mother's arms. But that was me. And that was who had I never wanted to be.

REDEPLOYMENT PACKING CHECKLIST
by Brooke King

CAMP LIBERTY, BAGHDAD, IRAQ
APRIL 2007

Pack your Army Combat Uniforms first. Military roll. Cram the black Under Armour sports bras, the tan undershirts, and the lucky convoy socks around the bottom inside edges of your green Army-issued duffle bag. Tuck the laminated photo into the bag, but don't look at it. You don't want to look at it. It's the picture that you held after your first recovery mission in the sand box, where you bagged and tagged three soldiers who had burned alive after their Stryker rolled over a pressure-plate IED. Your brother's smirk and your father's wide grin, your look of disenchantment, the picture taken when you were on R&R, all three of you standing in front of the house, each one of you pretending that nothing had changed since you left for Iraq. It helped you fall asleep that night. You can't help yourself. You unpack the photo to look at it once more. The corner edges are falling apart. The girl in the photo used to be you, but that's not the face you see in the mirror anymore.

Pack your camo-covered Army Bible. The pages have to be rubber-banded shut, otherwise it opens to Psalm 23. Pack your tan "Rite in the Rain" combat notebook, another sort of bible:

the name and rank of every soldier you ever placed into a black
body bag written on its pages. Poems. Letters to your father that
you never mailed. Pack the maroon prayer rug you stole while
raiding a house in Sadr City. Unpack the prayer rug. Kneel on
it while you pack the empty M4 magazines, the pistol holster,
ammo pouches, and desert combat boots. Pick up your aviator
gloves, the feel of manning the 50 cal machine gun on convoy.
Pick up the shell casing from your first confirmed kill. One of
six 7.62 caliber bullets that you fired into a fifteen-year-old boy's
chest. He was shooting an AK 47 at you. You shouldn't have the
shell casing. You shouldn't have the gloves. Women weren't supposed to see combat. Pack it all into the duffle.

Pack the hours spent in a cement bunker waiting for mortar
rounds to stop whistling into base. Pack the hate and the anger.
Pack the fear. Pack the shame and disenchantment for a job done
too well. Pack the back-to-back months spent going out on convoy without a day off. Pack your combat lifesaver bag, your hajji
killing license, and the rest of your dignity. Pack them all next
to the Army Core Values and the bullshit promise your government made to protect innocent civilians. Pack your worn copy
of Hemingway's The Sun Also Rises. Pack the tattered American
flag you picked up off the ground outside Abu Ghraib. Pack the
fucks and the goddamns tightly next to the it should've been me.
Pack the green duffle until there isn't room for anything else. Fold
over the top flaps. Shut it up tight. Lock it. Heave it onto your
back. Carry it all home.

AMBUSHED

by C. S. Griffin

T he Humvee headlights are weak. All I can see are the taillights of the enormous rig in front of me. The noise of the huge diesel engine combined with the tires treading heavily on the poorly maintained road, the wind coming in through the gaping hole in the roof. Conversation is impossible. It is usually cold in the desert at night. I am living on caffeine, nicotine and a fear in the back of my mind that something bad might happen if I don't pay attention. All I know is I still have several hours to my next destination.

Suddenly life is no longer real. It is more like I am just part of a big movie, no longer in control of anything going on, all action directed from someone off stage, and I am forced to watch frame-by-frame in slow motion as I act in one of the most important scenes of my life. Three men stand next to the road with rifles; they are firing at the vehicle in front of me. The flashes from the ends of the guns are so bright I can see the men's faces each time their weapons fire. Their images are tattooed on my brain as if my eyes were old-fashioned flashbulbs taking their portraits in a pitch black room. The projectiles they fire instantly report from their target and sparks fly everywhere.

My immediate thought is to wonder who in the hell would

be dumb enough to stand thirty feet from a military convoy and open fire. This could not really be happening. All logic flushes from my brain and my training kicks in. I never truly had any hope of controlling my actions. I realize that. My consciousness slips back to the recesses of my mind as the coursing adrenaline makes my voice powerful and reduces my motor skills to infantile capability.

"Contact left, Jumper 23, contact left; fire!" I scream with authority into the microphone my hand has brought to my face. My other hand reaches to my GPS to mark this exact spot as I drive through the kill zone. As a casual observer in all of this, my consciousness cannot only watch my own actions, but also has the ability to leisurely take in much more. I hear the turret click, click, click CLANG as it locks into position. Barreling into the kill zone, I wonder how well the alleged bullet proof glass would hold up. Immediately, I identify the enemies' weapons as the Kalashnikov 1947 model; as Clint Eastwood said in Heartbreak Hill, "They make a unique sound." It is the sound that has been the voice of battle worldwide since it's inception. It is the rifle that fires a heavy load through an abbreviated barrel. It has no spring to slow or dampen the recoil, which makes it violent and jarring. The sound it creates is not smooth and professional like its American and European contemporaries. Cruel and crass, it spits its ugly brood.

I find it interesting that I have the ability to muse on such things in the split second I drive through an ambush. The sound of my own vehicle's .50 caliber machine gun, which has become as much a part of the crew as any of the other soldiers, adds its booming bellow to the orchestra of war. Hell's bells must ring in tune with the thunderous destruction wrought by this weapon. The links that hold all the gun's bullets together fall from its belly and daintily skip and dance on the console beside me, each like the sound of a ring dropped on a marble floor.

Soon I am completely inside the kill zone. I realize that, because I hear the enemies' bullets hitting the truck. I squeeze my eyes shut as I hear the bullets strike. First the fender, a dull thud like someone hitting a fragment of iron with a hammer. This is a tedious repetition as it gets closer and closer to the cab. The first bullet strikes the glass of the windshield. The sound is terrifying, akin to heavy hail on a window. It pierces my ears while my heart is pierced by heavy doubt that the window will hold.

The hailstorm passes. The suspense is released.

I open my eyes, now back on the highway in San Antonio, scared to death and hyperventilating. My wife drives because she no longer trusts me with this mundane activity. I see my surroundings: road construction, jackhammers, road flares, grim men toiling at their work.

TOMATOES INSTEAD OF A PARADE

By Casondra Brewster

here is a ghost sitting at the desk in front of me. It
is still, dark, powdery, and charred to skeleton. I can
smell the fires still burning, jet fuel mixed with concrete
and new construction. All of it is now disintegrated.
There is the sound of smoldering echoing all around us. This is
no haunted fun house, no Halloween decoration. The calendar,
weirdly unmolested by the explosion, reads September.

I can't stop looking at the ghost, the shadow. I want to scream,
or vomit, or both. But nothing comes out. The smell, there are
no words for it, none, just revulsion deep in my stomach. There is
a blue searchlight, hot on my face now as if I'm on a stage. I feel as
if I'm simply caught in a bad horror flick. The light goes down towards my boots. It is my fellow sergeant. I can only view my comrade's eyes between engineer hard-hat cover and confined-space
breathing mask. His eyes are red and watery. It's clear our op has
changed from rescue to just recovery.

Then there is water from above. It's seeping in from where the
firefighters are still trying to put out the flames. Above me hover
clouds and some stars where the roof used to be. I feel it on my
face. It isn't just water, but also a chemical required to fight this
kind of intense blaze. The liquid is mixed with debris – building

and human alike.

I close my eyes. I pretend it's only rain washing away all the tragedy around me. I imagine I see the ghost as he looked before this grisly act. Tall, strong, a soldier's soldier coming home to throw the football with a son or teaching math to a daughter, dress blues at an evening gala ball with a proud spouse. I imagine him relaxing and sharing a well-earned brew with fellow soldier friends on a small patio while the bugle call of retreat echoes throughout post. But there is no coming home, no three-day pass, no annual leave, and no thank-you parade, nothing more for this ghost at the desk.

When I open my eyes, I don't see my battle buddy. In front of me is my yard, my garden, full of green, vibrant plants. It's nearly thirteen years from the day I lost my boots and uniform to jet fuel and other hazmat and biohazard contamination, my favorite pair of boots for which I still mourn. Those boots walked on soil from South Carolina to historic battlefields across Europe into Bosnia and Iraq and Macedonia and finally to the Pentagon. Every time rain hits my face, I'm back at that moment, staring at that ghost at its desk in the Pentagon, working on something no one knows or remembers.

I never learned his or her name. That's probably why it haunts me when it rains, like a collective grief that will never be put to rest no matter how many times taps floats through the air at the site of the attack.

A decade later, I was at my son's ball game. The rain started easy enough. It had been too warm; the precipitation was a welcome respite. I looked up. There, between home plate and first base, I saw that gray desk and black, ashy skeleton. The rain picked up. The skies darkened. No one noticed my tears.

I live in one of the rainiest places in the entire nation. It's a whole country away from the Pentagon. I remain here and I remember, even if I don't know the when-they-were-alive details. I plant poppies in one corner, for the ghost, and for all those I did know and lost that day and over the years, including the pre-attack me.

It's raining again today. For one split second with each Western Washington rain, jet-fuel soaked boots and charred skeleton in a chair are pulled from my being and laid into the earth, here in my garden, where the ghost's memory now grows tomatoes.

ANY STATION THIS NET
by Alex Flynn

P rivate Miller is eating a Pop-Tart now and later today he'll have watched two men die. Then he'll tear into dinner afterward like it's the last meal he'll ever have. His platoon sergeant, a veteran of inconceivable horrors in Iraq and Afghanistan, will remark, "It's so fucking weird man, every time these guys see death like that, they get hungry. I've never been able to figure that out."

Later that evening as the sun slowly dips below the horizon, with the staccato of small arms fire and tracer rounds arcing through the sky, he stands on the back ramp of a Stryker staring into nothing and says, to no one in particular, or maybe says to me since I was the only one staring at nothing with him, "I can't get the faces of all dead people I've seen out of my head." I'll be taken aback, and I won't know what to say so I'll try and joke, "That last guy didn't have a face, kid. Chill out." Then he'll snap out of it, giggling like the 19 or 20-year-old kid he is and we'll go back to talking about girls and booze and how it's bullshit that it's so cold and we're not allowed to build a fire. He'll ask me to email the pictures I took of him today. "My family would probably print 'em out," he says. "They're really proud."

* * *

I'm standing in the frozen food section of Sam's Club and I
hear the beeping sound of a forklift and I close my eyes and I'm
back. Back in Afghanistan; in freezing rain, lighting a cigarette,
and the second I spark my lighter I'm standing in a cloud of dust.
I can't breathe because my mouth is filled with grit and I can't
hear anything except a high-pitched ringing and my cigarette is
still burning on my lips and the thirteen-year-old boy I was following around a corner is convulsing on the ground in-front of
me. The nearby Afghan National Army soldiers are gone, pre-
sumably blown apart. I notice bits of their uniform stuck in a
nearby tree, fluttering in the breeze; which for a moment is the
most beautiful thing I've ever seen. But the kid, that poor kid,
his legs, jaw, and left arm are gone and I'm giggling because I'm
in shock and it looks like the kid is doing the worm but he's not.
He's in his death throes. It's dead quiet because the kid can't do
anything but make gurgling sounds as he fades and I hear one
of our vehicles reversing to pick him up and check on me and it
sounds just like the fucking forklift in Sam's Club and my girlfriend says, "Baby, are you alright?" and I shake it off and walk
toward the automotive section and buy new tires for my Subaru.
Nice tires, the most expensive all-weather tires I can buy because
I'm not fucking dying in a car accident.

WAKING UP FOR SCHOOL
by Samuel Abel

C rack.
The door to the helicopter locks to the open position. The latching sound resonates in time with the
throbbing of the rotors and the whine of the turbine
engine. A hot wind envelops my whole body and never goes
away. Neither does the earth and grit, like an old wool blanket
that you can't shake off.

Crack. Again the door locks opens. This time the sound in
my ears is louder, sharper. It lingers, beating to the drum of the
blades. The high-pitched screech is searching for the last corner
of my brain that hasn't been reached yet. I can feel my heart shaking my lungs as I dig deep for breath. Crack. I smell blood.

Crack.

Beep.

It's my alarm clock. I swallow to purge the copper taste that
still lingers from my dream. I am awake. The back of my neck is
stuck to my pillowcase. Sweat has locked it in place like a warm
palm on a frozen door handle in winter. Only willing to release if
applied with the right amount of pressure. I don't move. I don't
breathe. I listen for the sound of rotor blades. I listen for the whine
of churning engines. I listen. Beep. Only my alarm. I am awake.

I feel the heat of my body dissipating even as I swing mechanically for the alarm clock. It's autumn, and the timid cool of the season's change is discernible at this hour. I dread the moment my feet contact the cold bedroom floor, a relic of my childhood past. As a kid, morning was my time to dream, where I could linger in a state of hazy opportunity fantasizing about pulling off my first kickflip, or a lunchtime snack trade. Not having to exert any effort into completing the tasks ahead but rather relishing the certitude that, of course, everything would work out as designed.

The moment my feet hit the floor though, fantasy swiftly turns to reality and begrudgingly I must go forth to showers, breakfasts, bus rides to school, teachers, lunch lines, et cetera, et cetera. It's funny to me that I am still in school. It's fall and I am three weeks into my courses at community college. It has been eleven months and twenty four days since I left the military. Now in my second semester, my days are once again filled with the same activities of my childhood, only without innocence. Everything is different. Everything has changed.

I can feel my body trying to adapt to my conscious state, my anxiety snapping on and off like a broken lighter of a rusty grill as I ask myself the same question I ask myself every morning now, what are my goals, what is my mission? The nerves of youth have evolved into a crippling need for a plan. I must know every step required by my day now before I take it. Every event must be analyzed beforehand and every move taken deliberate. Nothing can be casually approached, because I know what complacency can do. I have seen it.

Shower, that is my first task of the day, although just getting out of bed will be tough. The security of my bed is known to me. The floor invites confusion, it invites chaos. The cramped shower is not inviting. The hot steam filling my lungs and constricting the blood vessels in my chest reminds me of boot camp, breathing in CS gas in a darkened room with one light above, mucus flowing from my nose, past my lips as they sound out my third general order. The beating of the water drops from the shower,

is rhythmic, dull, constant, like the rotors of the helicopter. Hot
air is swimming around my face. I am a product of that heat. I
have become it.

Crack.

Every drop of water slamming into the white acrylic bottom
of my bathtub is another helo door locking back. Another round
being fired downrange.

Crack. Crack.

The bullets fly.

Thump, thump.

The rotors turn.

And the hot, sticky water beading off my skin drips downward.
I smell blood.

Crack. The box of cereal lands on the countertop. It's breakfast time. Breakfast is no longer an enjoyable break in the morning routine, it is a function. My body is a machine, and a machine must have fuel to run. I know this. I know this because I
am a mechanic. I am a mechanic of the human body. And just
like a machine, the human body when it is broken can be fixed.
Just like the mechanic, the medic fixes it.

I can re-inflate the lung of a nineteen-year-old marine after
it has been pierced by a 7.62 millimeter round hurled from an
AK-47. Like a mechanic's, my hands work off muscle memory,
locating the entry site from the pool of blood collecting under the
cover of his BDU.

Listening for the muted gargle of air escaping his lungs.

Smelling the sweet copper stench of blood mixed with linger-
ing sulfur.

Watching pinkish bubbles foaming forth from the glistening
black hole in his chest, about the size of the milk bubbles collecting on the edges of my cereal bowl. One of them pops.

Crack. I drop my spoon.

What's next? To school, yes, I must plan my way to class. I have
to catch the number forty-four bus southbound from the bus stop,
sixty seven paces from my apartment. The bus leaves at 0843. I

must leave my apartment no later than 0836 to allow for any un-foreseen deviance in the schedule, because complacency kills.

Crack.

The door of the bus snaps open and I wait for a frail woman clutching a brown tote and a copy of the day's newspaper to dis-embark.

I wait, listening to the whine of the bus engine, smelling hot fumes reeking of petroleum.

A hydraulic valve releases a hiss like it's whispering at me.

Like the hiss of the stretcher as the medical team raises the bed up level with the helicopter door, ready to be ridden by a nineteen year old marine.

As ready as he was for his first ride in the car his parents bought him when he turned sixteen.

That is how ready I must be today.

Ready to ride that bus.

Ready for anything to happen.

Ready for that moment, just after the crack, when the tires start shrieking, and the glass starts breaking, and the metal starts twisting and tearing.

Metal propelled haphazardly through the air, racing, twirling, searching.

Seeking out a lung for it to perforate.

Always you must be ready for an IED, because complacency kills.

I am awake.

And now what, after the bus?

I must know this before my feet hit the ground.

Even before my bedtime sanctuary is abandoned.

As a child, getting ready for school was much more linear.

I made sure I had my lunch, my books, my homework. I tried not to forget my sweatshirt in my locker. I'd try to get picked for the good team during kickball at lunch.

Now I must try not to get picked for anything at all. I try not to draw any more attention to myself than I already do, five years senior to my average classmate and with my arms branded in military tattoos.

In Iraq it was never good to stand out. In Iraq we wore combat boots to support our ankles, to protect our feet, to kick down doors.

Now I choose footwear that makes the least amount of noise as they batter against the linoleum floor of the classroom.

My legs churn up and down, pumping like the pistons of a turbine engine, my heels launching and landing with a rhythmic thud on the cold ground.

I can hear the rotors.

I smell the chemicals used by the morning janitor to wipe the floors clean.

The smell of the chemicals used to wash the blood from the floor of the tent hospital. I can feel the hair on my arms rise up as I think of the tension in that casualty-receiving bay.

The confusion, chaos, the noise and the movement.

Like walking through the courtyard on campus.

Everyone going somewhere.

Everyone doing something.

What is my something.

What is my mission now?

To get home.

To leave this school that reeks of ammonia and blood.

This campus that's teeming with people that I don't know, whose missions are a mystery to me.

Yes, I must get home to my bed, my sanctuary, to sleep. I need more sleep. Crack. The textbook on the desk next to mine slams shut. Class is over, it's time to go home.

Home. Yes, it is time to go home.

Time to go to my apartment, sixty seven paces from the forty-four bus stop.

It is time to come home, in, out of the throbbing heat. In from the gritty air that smells of JP-5 and rubber.

Yes, it is time to come home. To come back to a life of friends and family, safety and comfort, kickball and paper bag lunches.

I come home to my apartment, and my marines are there waiting for me, laughing, drinking. All of them, stuffed into my shabby living room as if we we're back at the barracks ogling the new boot's Facebook pictures of his girlfriend back home.

All of us there, even the ones who didn't come home.

But no, that is not right. That is not home. That is just a dream, a hazy half-memory of a time before. A flickering thought of what would never be.

My home is my bed, my blankets. There I am safe. There I am home.

I am alone.

I am awake.

Crack.

My feet touch the bedroom floor.

HOMECOMING II
by Brent Wingfield

A
s I trudged through Afghanistan's lush Mizan River Valley on what would be my final combat patrol, I stopped momentarily to catch my breath before climbing out of a knee-deep canal and over an earthen embankment. I wanted to keep my guys out of the river bed where we were easy targets, and off the roads where the locals liked to bury explosives. They didn't usually like placing the IED's in or around their homes, so to hell with the roads, I thought.

We took the safest route: through their fields and farms. None of us wanted to be the latest casualty in a forgotten war, and no one was trying to be a hero, especially on our last mission. I stopped and relayed instructions via radio to my two team leaders. I told them to start maneuvering their fire teams towards me; we were taking a detour.

I took a deep breath and scaled the retaining wall. When I reached the top, I looked at the fields ahead. An acre of red poppies danced playfully in the breeze as the craggy mountains cast a looming shadow over some mud-walled homes ahead. I marveled as the Afghan cliffs slowly swallowed the most beautiful sunset I had ever seen.

"It'd be kinda pretty if it weren't for all those shitty houses,"

Guenther's voice came from over my shoulder.

Brian "Hans" Guenther was one of my team leaders and closest friends. Though I outranked him, Hans was twelve years my senior. He was like an older brother. I met eyes with the mustachioed man, smiled and looked back to the sunset.

"It's beautiful," I paused, "but tainted." The lush valley was a light show of colors, littered with crude, mud-walled houses, dirt roads and the scars of centuries of war. I was captivated. The views were tremendous, but I was sick of seeing them at the same time. I missed my home, my wife, and my pug, Roxy. I missed having a beer after work. My gut wrenched over the decision I knew that I had to make, a decision that I knew was long overdue.

But I wasn't sure if I was ready, or even wanted to hang up my boots and say goodbye to life as an infantryman. After a seven-year-long love-hate relationship with the Army, most of which was spent overseas, I realized that I loved seeing the world and the camaraderie and the experience of serving, but I had long-since grown weary of the caveats.

I was at the end of my enlistment and had to make a choice: re-up or get out. I wanted to stay in but I was tired. I was tired of saying goodbye to my wife, tired of keeping my family at a distance, and I was tired of keeping a guilty tab on my growing list of dead friends. I longed for a "normal" life, even though I didn't have any idea what the hell that even meant. I just knew that it had to be better than all this.

But on the other hand, I loved what I did. Training soldiers and leading them through combat was the most rewarding experience of my life. I loved the guys with whom I served like family, and being a grunt was all I had known since I was nineteen. I wondered if I should just accept the fact that this was my life. I looked around. Maybe I should learn to love this, I thought.

I turned to Guenther and his friendly eyes cut through me. He knew me.

"Let's get ready to move," I told him.

"Take us home Sergeant," Guenther said with a friendly wink.

I nodded and smiled. "I'll stay on point," I said. "We'll head through that farm at our two-o'clock and link up with the rest of the platoon ahead." We bumped knuckles and I started walking backwards.

"Roger. We'll follow." Guenther said. He turned and walked off to relay instructions to bravo team.

I kept walking backwards, admiring the soldiers in my squad. Damnit, I am gonna miss this, I thought as I watched them following in formation. It had taken countless hours of training and a year at war to turn what was once a gaggle-fuck of misfits and teenagers into an effective and cohesive fighting force. I smiled proudly as I watched them climb from the canal and into the poppy field. I turned and started walking to check ahead for sight of 1st Squad.

As I stepped, I twisted my ankle and ate shit. Gravity jerked my body one way, and sent the 90 pounds of gear I was wearing violently in the opposite direction. I sailed to the ground like a bag of bricks and apparently, it was quite the sight. Laughter erupted behind me.

"Fuckin' A," I said and threw my hands up, laughing at myself. What could I do? I brushed mud from my face and struggled back to my feet.

As I stood, I caught sight of the lead squad. My Platoon Sergeant Tony Robb was standing with them atop a large, brown hill. I looked through my binoculars and saw him staring at me. His face was red with laughter. Apparently everyone had noticed my fall.

"You alright?" Robb half giggled into his radio.

"This shit'll buff out," I answered into my mine.

"Aren't you gonna miss all this Wingnut?" Robb's Tennessee drawl cackled through my radio's muddy mic. Wingnut, I thought. He knew I hated that.

"Fuck no," I answered, still spitting out pieces of Afghanistan as I spoke.

I adjusted my gear and noticed an Afghan family standing

outside their mud hovel. A small, brightly dressed girl with long, dark hair waved and smiled. She made me think of my cousin. Two men stood beside the girl, staring silently. I looked at the poppies I had smashed and shrugged. They were pissed. I dusted myself off and kept moving.

Guenther's fire-team was quickly approaching from behind. "Watch these guys, Hans," I motioned in the direction of the men.

"We've got eyes on," Guenther affirmed.

I reached the edge of the scarlet morphine farm and climbed a wall to the next one. I could see pink and white poppies planted in neat rows in the next field. As I climbed, my mind wandered back to scaling walls while fighting house-to-house in Southern Baghdad years prior.

It wasn't anything like this.

Back then, we would quickly climb crude walls, rush into half-ruined homes, and fight our way to the rooftops. Entire neighborhoods would erupt into gunfire and my heart would race as I clutched my rifle's grip, my eyes and sights racing frantically through the haze of incoming lead. I remembered the confusion of trying to tell which civilians were just trying not to get shot and which ones were trying to kill us; we rarely could.

I thought of the adrenaline rush as bullets sang overhead and I remembered the piercing cries from those that struck true. I remembered the ever-present, carnivorous dread that gnawed at our sanity, and I remembered how we fought through it arrogantly.

I thought of the dozen guys that didn't make it home and the couple dozen more who got fucked up, blown up or shot. I remembered how the rest of us were left to carry on and fight in their absence and I remembered how we tried to pick up the pieces of our lives when we went home.

The dead are the lucky ones.

I was still coming to terms with my first homecoming from war on the eve of leaving Afghanistan. I relived old firefights by night and avoided them by day. I was neurotic about my guys' safety, because I was tired of seeing young Americans die on forgotten battlefields, in wars no one back home gave a shit about anymore.

Fuck this, I thought.

But as I heaved my body over a final barrier and walked towards our combat outpost, my mood changed. I led my squad through the second poppy field and onto a small dirt road leading towards our mountain home. After a day spent battling the crags and valleys, I walked the last few painful, muddy steps smiling because I knew that at least this time, it was all different.

I took a heavy breath and smiled.

I knew that I was still dealing with some old demons, but at least I had managed to keep my shit together. I had trained and led ten soldiers through twelve months of combat, and this time, I was bringing all of them home alive, and most of them were still in one piece.

I had done my job well and I was proud.

I stopped at the entrance to our sandbagged outpost and kicked most of the mud from my boots. I looked at the faces of my soldiers and counted them as they walked through the concertina wire. I smiled with every passing face. "Awesome job guys."

I keyed my mic for the last time: "Hey Two-Six, Two-Three. We're a hundred percent."

"Roger that Two-Three. Welcome home," I heard my Lieutenant's voice answer through the radio.

Guenther waited for me. He and I entered last. "My feet are barking," he said.

"That's 'cause you're too old for this shit," I teased.

"Fuck you, Sergeant," he said with a smile. We bumped helmets affectionately.

"Come on, let's go get some chow," I said.

* * *

The next day, I again counted my guys as they boarded a CH-47 helicopter. It was our ride out of the bomb-laden mountains and back to Camp Disneyland, otherwise known as Kandahar Airfield, or KAF. KAF was our next stop on our way back home to Germany, where we were stationed.

"Going home" never felt real until the CH-47 threw massive plumes of dirt up as we lifted off the mountainside and flew south. We were so close to finally leaving Asscrackistan and we all looked forward to the families, booze, and brothels that awaited. I remembered my first awkward homecoming, and I wondered how many years it would take to "adjust" this time. I closed my eyes and listened to the helicopter clamor through the desert dawn.

I thought of red poppies.

Later that night, Robb Guenther and I went out to explore our interim home. Compared to our forsaken outpost, KAF was a 5-star resort, and we fully intended to enjoy ourselves. The three of us went and bought some cigars and a pizza to celebrate our deployment's end.

We reminisced about humping our gear over mountains, getting rained on and eating expired MREs, all while the assholes stationed on KAF had such plush living conditions. The leviathan air base had USO shows, PX's and contractor-run dining facilities. There was a weekly "Salsa Night" on the Boardwalk, an actual boardwalk lined with shops and restaurants.

"Afghanistan: individual experiences may vary," I joked as I chewed pepperoni pizza.

"Seriously, is it a deployment or a vacation for these fuckin' guys?" Guenther said.

Our twelve months in Afghanistan had truly sucked, and in confounding new ways nonetheless, but my experiences had paled in comparison to the combat I'd seen in Iraq years prior. I remembered seeing burned homes, dead kids, and friends lose limbs. I felt stupid for complaining.

"I'm just happy we got everybody here," I said.

"Those soldiers of yours," Tony Robb looked to me and said. "Brand, Espinoza, Spaulding…"

"Yeah, they sure didn't make it easy," I nodded.

"No, they didn't," Guenther agreed. We had been like dads to the guys of our squad. Over the last year, we had walked them through everything from weapons training to personal hygiene issues.

"Yeah, we're all still alive," I said. "In spite of stubborn soldiers…"

"Lazy Sergeants…" Robb teased.

"And the most valiant efforts of our chain of command" I said.

"You ain't kiddin'" he nodded.

The three of us sat, chewing our food in silence for several minutes. It was nice to finally enjoy the fruits of society again. A greasy pizza and a Coke. I was in heaven.

And that's when Robb's phone rang. It was one of the soldiers in our platoon. Guenther shot me a worried glance. We could hear the panicked voice. Something had happened back at our platoon's tents, something terrible.

Robb's brow curled sharply as he listened to the frantic soldier. "It's Spaulding," Robb told us as his gut visibly sank. "Spaulding's been shot."

"He was shot?" Guenther's voice cracked.

Shot? It didn't make any sense; we were miles away from any real combat, on the eve of our homecoming.

Robb looked at Guenther and I. "We need to go!"

We scrambled to our feet and out the door. Robb clutched his phone and rifle as he ran. My heart raced. "They're there now?" he said into the phone. "Good. We'll meet them at the hospital. I'll be back at the tent as soon as I can," he assured the soldier and hung up.

"Stop that bus," Robb motioned and yelled.

Guenther and I stepped into the road and tried to flag-down a passing bus. It didn't stop, so we raised our rifles. After looking down the business end of two carbines, the driver slammed the vehicle to an immediate halt and the three of us climbed aboard. Guenther and I sat in the first row and Robb informed the driver where to go: the ER.

"Now, what the hell happened?" Guenther asked.

Robb took a deep breath. "All I managed to hear was that

Spaulding's been shot and that Baker did it," Robb told us as he sat, his tone more of a question.

Baker was another soldier in our platoon and a close friend of Spaulding, and although they were both problem soldiers, none of this added up.

"That doesn't make any sense," I said.

"He said something about... they were playing," Robb's face cringed, "and that Baker shot him in the head."

"What the fuck?" Guenther said.

The bus dropped us off at the Combat Support Hospital exactly as the Humvee arrived that was carrying our wounded soldier, Riley Spaulding. His face was covered in blood-drenched gauze. I could see that he had suffered a point-blank gunshot wound to the forehead. My mind raced with questions. The reasons why were still fuzzy; the trauma was all that was clear.

I watched four Corpsmen carry Riley Spaulding onto a hospital bed and quickly wheel him inside. Robb, Guenther, and I followed closely. As they pushed the gurney through a doorway, Spaulding's bandage fell from his face.

He's not gonna make it, I thought.

We watched the frantic doctors do what they could. They tried their damndest but it was no use. It was too late. I looked at the bullet hole in Riley's forehead. It was too much.

God damnit.

Robb and Guenther headed back to be with the rest of our platoon while I stuck around to fill out the necessary paperwork. What the fuck Spaulding? I looked at his vacant eyes. You were trained better than this!

What the fuck were you doing?

I choked back tears as I signed my name, officiating his death. He was a lovable goof, kind of like a little brother.

And now he was dead.

A week later, we were all back in Germany. We landed at Rammstein Air Base near Frankfurt, and then loaded buses on our way back to Vilseck where our lives that were interrupted a year prior had left off.

As the bus drove on the Autobahn I stared out my window at the thick, green pines and ferns and rain-soaked roads. I didn't know what to think about the carefree civilians driving beside us. They were completely oblivious. It was odd to not worry about IEDs in the road. It was weird to be so close to home. Suddenly, it wasn't such a vague concept.

I thought of what it was like going home last time and I shuddered. I wondered what it would be like now. This time, everything was different.

I thought about Riley Spaulding.

We were less than an hour away.

PROGRESS NOT PERFECTION
by Gill Sotu

Progress not perfection
I am coming home...
I learned what I could
Saluted who I had to,
and ate what they fed me

If I never see another chicken fried steak on a plastic pink tray
    I'd die a happy man.
I'm ready for the sun to know me by my first name again
Tired of adapting,
I have never been good at playing ocean
This tree has roots that long to be planted
Progress not perfection
I'm coming home...

I remember leaving,
I remember the party they threw in honor of me sailing off to
    protect this country
Not much fanfare in succeeding safely.
Coming home is not as fancy
Much like a divorce, people just want to know what's next

And saying "I don't know" is like checking "other" when asked
   to list your ethnicity
America doesn't do vague
If we can't label it, it doesn't exist
4 years and no real combat,
I always get the question,
"Are you really a veteran?"...YES!

My time served wasn't idyllic
I may have missed a few musters
I may have wrote a few poems when I should have been watch-
   ing out for the enemy...
One or two may have slipped by in the middle of a stanza...
But I put on my patriotism one leg at a time just like the deco-
   rated, the wounded, the forgotten...
None of us, perfect soldiers, sailors, marines
None of us, perfect fathers, wives, husbands, nieces, or sons
but all of us...
have to come home, or find a new one.

Do not expect us to return better
Just be open
Do not expect us to return stronger
Just be open
Do not expect us to return understanding what happened to the
   world in our absence...
Just be open...
And we will always love you for it.
Progress not perfection
We are coming home

WELCOME HOME
by Doug D'Elia

"The return from war should be a solemn experience."
                                        --Captain Andrew Miller

They say that when Jesus' body
was taken down from the tree
and moved to the cave,
God darkened the sky
for three hours that all could
begin sitting Shiva, the Hebrew
tradition of mourning the dead.

In Nam we never had
time to mourn the dead.
They were evacuated quickly,
while we lay down cover.
Between bullets there
was a service and I thought
of them, but I couldn't
let my guard down. I didn't mourn.

And when I left that country,

the well wishers were waiting,
standing in the bright of day
with stuffed animals,
waving hand-held American flags,
and shaking our trembling hands.
And as I looked into their naïve eyes
I see the strangers I have killed,
men and woman, and some children
that wandered into my line of fire.

God forgive me! Darken the sky
again that I may sit Shiva in the
seclusion of my room with
wax candles and mirrors covered
with my torn clothes.
Let my tears flow like rivers
as I recite Psalms to each soldier
who died in my arms, and let
the wind hear my pain
and whisper, Welcome home.

49 STEPS TO OWNING A SERVICE DOG

by Tenley Lozano

1. Join the military at 17 to serve your country and as a way to get a college degree without debt. Serve nine years and seven months on Active Duty.

2. Separate from the military as soon as your commitment is complete, in order to get away from frequent deployments. And even more frequent harassment.

3. Realize that your experiences in the military affected you in ways you don't understand; you've kept away from situations where men are drinking because you can't relax, you've been avoiding crowds for months because the anxiety of being around all those people triggers migraines, and you get jumpy when a strange man stands too close behind you in line for coffee.

4. Visit local animal shelters to pick out a dog for a new running and hiking buddy now that you won't have to worry about short-notice deployments. Chose one that is athletic, high-energy, with intelligent eyes and a tendency to lick your fingers and face. A volunteer at the shelter will say in a high-pitched tone, "Oh, you're adopting Princess! She's such a beautiful dog. We rescued her from a shelter up north the day she was going to be put down. Then we brought her here and she was adopted by a couple that kept her in a kennel for eight to ten hours a day until

she chewed out of it and destroyed their house. They returned her after a week. So she might have some issues." Immediately change her name from "Princess" to something more fitting for a real dog.

5. Read online about Service Dogs for veterans and decide to start training your rescue dog. You're not sure if you need a Service Dog or not, but you know you need help and if you decide not to use her as a Service Dog you figure you'll just have an extremely obedient pet.

6. Visit the VA Hospital to start your Disability Benefits for tinnitus, caused by hours working underwater as a diver where sound is amplified, and receive a US Department of Veterans Affairs ID card.

7. Learn that it is possible to have a disability rating for a psychiatric disorder.

8. Admit to yourself that you've suffered with depression and anxiety for years, but hid it from your co-workers and medical record under the fear of losing your job in the military.

9. Learn that there is a Mental Health Floor in the VA Hospital with walk-in spots to see a psychiatrist. Bring your Service Dog In-Training because you will need her, you will be in tight spaces with many other veterans and she may be the only thing preventing you from having a panic attack.

10. Focus on your dog. When you sit in the mental health waiting area under the buzzing fluorescent lights, she will sit obediently at your feet, completely relaxed, with her attention on you. VA Hospital workers will smile at you and say, "Your dog is so well behaved." A man in his 50s with a shaggy beard will stand in the corner of the waiting area talking loudly. He will say, "There's not supposed to be dogs here. It's a hospital. No dogs in the hospital. Why's there a dog. No dogs allowed. She's got a dog. No dogs allowed. Why's nobody kicking out her dog. No fucking dogs!"

11. Ignore this man.

12. Sit down in the psychiatrist's office. She will ask you, "So

you're here for medication?"

13. Tell her that you don't want meds.

14. Tell her that you want a prescription for a Service Dog.

15. Explain to her what a Service Dog is.

16. Learn that sexual harassment, sexual assault, and rape fall under the title of Military Sexual Trauma.

17. Receive referral to the Military Sexual Trauma and Interpersonal Trauma Clinic of the VA Healthcare System.

18. Schedule appointment for Mental Health Orientation Meeting at the local VA clinic in two months.

19. Memorize the definition of a Service Dog listed in the Americans with Disabilities Act: "Service Animals are defined as dogs that are individually trained to do work or perform tasks for people with disabilities."

20. Know your access rights: Under the ADA, businesses that serve the public must allow service animals to accompany people with disabilities in all areas of the facility where the public is normally allowed to go.

21. Know that staff of a store may ask only two questions when they see you with your Service Dog:

Is the dog required because of a disability?

And: What task has the dog been trained to perform?

22. Be sure to keep your response vague when answering questions about your Service Dog, to avoid telling what your disability is and being discriminated against. Do not announce, "My Service Dog is trained to watch behind me when I have to stand with my back to other people, she blocks people from getting too close to me and triggering anxiety attacks, and she also guards me and licks me when I have an anxiety attack." Instead, say, "My Service Dog alerts to my medical condition."

23. Attend Mental Health Orientation at the local VA Clinic.

24. Following orientation, meet with yet another psychiatrist.

25. Sit down in the psychiatrist's office. She will ask you, "So you're here for medication?"

26. Tell her that you don't want meds. Tell her that you want

a prescription for a Service Dog. Explain to her what a Service Dog is.

27. Listen closely as the psychiatrist recommends that you attend therapy sessions. She will tell you that it will be several months before you can get an appointment for an individual therapy session. "You're better off signing up for the group therapy sessions. We start the groups in cycles so it looks like you'll have to wait three months until the next ones start. We can sign you up now and call you before the group meets."

28. Sign up for the anxiety group therapy sessions. Do not expect a phone call. You will not receive a phone call.

29. Make appointment to see the physician assistant in two weeks.

30. Sit down in the physician assistant's office. He will ask you, "So you're here for medication?"

31. Tell him that you don't want meds. Tell him that you want a prescription for a Service Dog. Explain to him what a Service Dog is.

32. Receive prescription for a Medical Alert Service Dog to assist with your diagnosed PTSD.

33. Contact non-profit organization Train A Dog, Save A Warrior to receive funding for Service Dog training. The man who answers the phone will say, "How long were you in the military for? Don't you think you deserve free Service Dog training for everything you went through?"

34. Complete application for the program, including multiple character references, mental health questionnaires, letters of recommendation from the VA physician assistant, and prescription for Service Dog. You will be accepted into the program and they will contact local trainers to find one who will work with you and your dog.

35. Don't get your hopes up about free Service Dog training. All local organizations will refuse to work with a PTSD Service Dog, claiming that they only train mobility dogs.

36. Continue training your dog on your own, paying for les-

sons with your own money.

37. Put a vest on your dog that makes her easily identifiable as a Service Dog.

38. Never put your dog's name on a vest or collar that other people can easily read. They will shout your Service Dog's name and try to distract her.

39. You can add a patch that says "Disabled Veteran."

40. Be prepared to answer questions such as, "How is the dog a Disabled Veteran? Was she in combat in Iraq?" and "Bless you, honey. What organization are you training the dog for? I could never do that, train a dog and give it away."

41. Explain to strangers that the Service Dog is, in fact, for you, and that you are the Disabled Veteran. Expect the stranger to become confused, and then the next question will be, "Oh, so you have PTSD?"

42. Politely explain that it is actually extremely rude to ask a stranger about her medical history.

43. When people ask to pet your dog, say one of two things: "Not right now, she's working," or "Sure, she's friendly. Thank you for asking." Chose which one to say based on how focused you need your Service Dog to be at the moment. If she's being touched by strangers, she won't be paying as much attention to you.

44. Expect Drive-By Pettings and people whistling and calling to your dog when in public places.

45. Respond to this unwanted behavior by saying, "Please don't do that, she's working right now." Sometimes people will apologize. Sometimes they will yell at you or mumble under their breath, "Fucking cunt!" Ignore them.

46. Always bring a collapsible water bowl with you. Train your dog to pee and poop on command, and on grass, dirt, concrete, and AstroTurf.

47. When applying for jobs and interviewing, do not mention your Service Dog or disability until you have an offer. If it looks like you're about to get a job offer and you try to be open with the company, wanting to work for an organization that ac-

cepts you and your Service Dog as a team, do not expect any further correspondence about the job.

48. Try leaving your dog at home even when you know you'll be working in a small crowded room. Realize that you do need your Service Dog to help you focus, prevent migraines, and stop panic attacks.

49. Strangers will say, "That's so great that you get to take your dog with you everywhere!" Smile and think to yourself sarcastically, "Maybe one day they'll be so lucky!"

HOMEWARD BOUND

by Jim Ruland

T he day I got out of the Navy, I walked down the gang-
plank with a seabag slung over my shoulder and two
thoughts on my mind: USN, never again. And that
went double for San Diego.

I had my reasons: Inflexible discipline. Stifling conformity.
Rules. I hated the way the Navy tried to squeeze every bit of individuality out of me. Just another piece of government property
to be put in harm's way.

To blow off steam, I'd hit the streets of San Diego, but there
was nowhere to go. I didn't have a car to go to the beach. The
Gaslamp hadn't been invented yet. I'd go to Horton Plaza, get a
lemonade from Hot Dog on a Stick, fill it with gin, and try to
meet girls at the mall. But the thing about being a sailor in a sailor
town is that people treat you like some unruly creature that only
wants to fuck, fight, and get drunk. All of which was more or less
true. But still...

In San Diego, sailors are treated like transients, like fruit pick-
ers or carnies. That left Tijuana, a place where sailors were routine-
ly hustled, robbed, assaulted. Like my shipmate Dwayne who got
jumped in the alley, hit in the face with a bottle and lost an eye.
A regular Popeye the sailor. Except that was the end of Dwayne's

adventures in the fleet. He was discharged and sent home.

I couldn't wait to be done with San Diego. When that day finally came, I went all the way across the country to a college 2,500 miles away.

But life has a way of making you revisit the assertions of your youth. Because I did come back to San Diego to get married. And now I live here. Every night I lay my head down just few miles from the Navy Station. I'd be hard pressed to get any closer to the place I swore I'd never back to. How did this happen?

My mother has a theory. She came out to visit a few summers ago. My wife Nuvia and I took her out to dinner at a restaurant in Coronado. We watched boats go by on the bay as the sun went down. It made her nostalgic for when she, too, lived in San Diego.

That was back in 1967. My father was stationed at North Island for swift boat training. They wanted to be together before he was shipped off to Vietnam. They splurged and rented a beachfront apartment they couldn't afford. And that's where I was conceived. Right there on the beach. Right here in San Diego. According to my mother, that's why I keep coming back. Like salmon swimming back to their home waters.

The Pacific salmon are strong swimmers. It's not uncommon for them to swim from California to the Sea of Japan. Some make this journey several times in their lifetime. But they always come back. You could say it's their destiny. An ancient memory encoded in their DNA.

After dinner (which I'm happy to report did not include salmon) we went in search of this magical place where I was hatched. A place called Imperial Beach. Only there was one problem: I have a terrible sense of direction. I frequently get lost, often very close to home. I can almost always be counted on to take the wrong exit, make the wrong turn. I use the GPS on my phone to get to places I've been to dozens of times.

But what does that mean exactly? What does it mean to get turned around? Why do I have such poor instincts for finding my way home? Easy, I inherited them from my mother. We're directionally challenged. And now we were chasing a 44-year-old memory.

Although I've learned not to trust my mother when it comes to directions, on the way to Imperial Beach she swore she remembered her old address. It was adjacent to a bar that billed itself as the most southwestern saloon in all of the United States.

"The IB Forum?" my wife asked.

My mother didn't remember. But Nuvia has an interesting story about the place. After breaking up with some loser, she went into the IB Forum to drown her sorrows. A friend of hers was learning how to bartend and she got Nuvia ridiculously drunk. U2 came on the jukebox and this resulted, as it often does, in a long crying jag. She went outside and shouted at the stars.

"When am I going to find the man for me?" Then she threw up in the parking lot. Little did she know that her future husband was conceived a few steps away.

While Nuvia told this story, I struggled with the GPS. Something wasn't right. As we crept down the strand looking for the building, I realized the apartment numbers were off. Way off. Like by a thousand. And the street name wasn't right. My mother insisted it looked familiar, which meant we were probably going to end up in TJ. When we passed IB Forum, my mother pointed to an apartment building and shouted, "That's it!"

I looked at the iPhone. We'd plugged in the wrong address and the wrong street, and it guided us right to this spot. Weird. Spooky even.

It was getting late, nearly dark. The apartments all looked the same. But my mother walked right in as if 44 years hadn't passed. She pointed out how the laundry room was on one side of the courtyard and the entrance to the beach on the other. And there they were.

The three of us went around the building to the beach. I was struck by how close to the ocean we were. The sound of the crashing surf filled our ears. Evening fog rolled in dampening our clothes and leaving a salty film on the rocks and railings.

"Here it is," she said. "This is where we lived. This is where you were conceived."

Suddenly, it all clicked. Being summoned to San Diego by the Navy when I was still a kid. All those journeys back and forth across the country, all those temporary addresses. It seemed like such a wayward way to build a life, a series of journeys without rhyme or reason. But from the perspective of the Pacific Salmon it made perfect sense. This is where I was spawned. This is where I returned to make a family. In spite of not knowing where I was going, my instincts kicked in and guided me home.

GRADUATION
by Zack Dryer

The second time that Ryan went to rehab after we got out of the Army, he called me every afternoon at twelve thirty. He was supposed to have a sobriety partner for one-on-one therapy work so he nominated me. And though the nurses, doctors, and security personnel told him that he had to choose from within his group, and I said no—partly because the doctor told me to, but also because I wasn't sober myself—Ryan can be persistent. So when the rest of the partners had their "break-away" time after morning group, Ryan called me from the doctor's office.

"Hey there, fuckface."

I was eating lunch with an old professor and some of his students on campus. I had discussed with Dr. Cox beforehand that I was expecting a call so when my phone vibrated I just nodded politely, slipped my chair under the long mahogany table, and headed for the door. Dr. Cox smiled, waved, and then continued on another of his famous lunchtime literature lectures—this time on the, "plethora of amazing contemporary fiction coming out of the Native American community."

"Well good day to you too, Dr. Jenkins, " I said, bringing the phone up to my ear as I pushed my way through the ancient carved doors into the dim grey afternoon. "I've been waiting on

your call—" the heavy wooden door settled shut with a thud,
"—fuckface."

"What's up, Georgey?"

"Nothing much. What's up with you?"

"Oh, you know, just calling to let you know how wonderful
it is here in New York."

"I'm sure."

There were a few scattered students sitting at the metal picnic
tables outside. On any other day every courtyard on the Texas
campus would be full of nervous freshmen and impatient se-
niors. Today it was almost empty. A girl in a light blue rain slicker
looked up at me under the overhang. Her eyes were crystal grey.

"Today is kinda nice actually, just a bit cold but the nurses
said they're gonna give out double servings of warm tapioca later
on and then we're in for another evening engagement with the
famous Rev. Roy Williams and his racially-diverse group of sym-
pathetic ex-smackhead finger puppets in the main hall."

"Sounds exciting?"

I could hear him rifling around through the doctor's desk.
"You bet your ass it's not exciting, Georgey. But I'll tell you what,
some of these mother fuckers in here seriously get wrapped up in
this shit like it was Days of our Fucking Lives—there are some
seriously checked-out mother fuckers in here, brother."

I could picture him in his cloth gown digging around in the
drawers and filing cabinets for anything useful or tradable with
the old, black receiver pinched up to his ear.

"Sounds rough."

"Oh, yeah, brother. This ain't one of those Army detoxes I
used to go to—this is the real shit here. There's this one old-tim-
er in here, Willie, on his nineteenth go round, fourteenth court
ordered. He, no bullshit, just drools all over himself during the
puppet shows and shit—Vietnam vet—nice guy to talk to when
he's lucid though—musta killed like a thousand gooks he says."

"Well at least you got somebody to talk to, right?"

"Yeah, he's a real doll. There's another vet, too--Durden—

don't drool near as much—only med time really."

"Nam?"

"Nope, Iraq."

"Oh, well see there, now you have two people to talk to. That's nice."

"Yeah, great." I heard the blinds go up and could sense him looking out the window at the early snow on the Adirondacks to the East and Iraq beyond them. The receiver was silent.

"Well at least you have company this time," I said, out loud to the empty sidewalk on the way to my car.

He was somewhere else for a moment. I stopped at the campus turtle pond and watched the red-eared sliders peacefully perching on their lily pads. A startled one slipped off into the shallow, murky water. He came back. "…Yeah, and he's even more fucked in the head than I am. Which is always nice."

"Who?"

"Durden—the Iraq vet."

"Oh, sorry. I was lost for a minute. How?"

"Got hit with a fucking RPG sitting in the back of a truck full of 40mm grenades—got blown to holy shit."

"Jesus," I cringed. I tried not to picture it. I'd been practicing for a little over four years and could almost not remember sometimes when I focused. No luck. "I meant how is he more messed up in the head than you?"

"Oh, he was full on spun out for like two years, bro. He's from somewhere up near Boston. Get this, so this fucker is sitting in the back of a truck on some convoy he just hopped on, right? Just trying to get back to his unit after mid-tour leave and he's a medic so he's got his bag with him and they stick him in this truck sitting on top of a pile of fucking ammo and supplies and a damn RPG hits right in the middle of that shit—BLAM! Grenades all go. BOOM! BOOM! BOOM! Smoke everywhere. Everything all blowing to high shit and all and he's sitting right in the middle of this. He's hit bad right—holes the size of fist through his legs and shit—and then this mother fucker treats his fucking self like some kind of Dr. Fucking Rambo with a ten foot pecker—calls his own vitals in to the medevac over the radio."

"Jesus."

"Right? Anyway gets packed up and shipped to Germany for six, seven months. Medals all pinned to a fresh uniform in his footlocker and shit. Then a year at Walter Reed—all the while they're feeding him a steady supply of the good shit, then BLAM—back to his unit for out-processing without even so much as a refill script, brother. Guy's damn near blowing hobos under the bridge for dope money in a week flat."

"Jesus, rough week."

"Yeah, then he ends up in and outta like three Army rehabs but the kid couldn't hardly tell up from down at this point, the monkey's so far up his ass, and they they just boot him—no money, no medal, no handshake—just scram."

"Jesus. Did he fight it?"

"Yeah, he's good now. His parents called the state senator or some shit, got fancy lawyers and good doctors and shit. They pay him now but he just shoots it, snorts it, drinks it all up, fucks it all away— you know."

"Yeah, I know." I was looking up at the clock tower feeling guilty about wishing it would strike one as I got to my car, and the rain started coming in earnest. "Well, at least he's getting the help he needs now, right?"

"Shit yeah, man. Hell it's been good to him too, bro. Even got himself a little blonde-headed girlfriend in here."

"Another patient?"

"Nope, even better—nurse Amanda. I tell you, brother— we're getting all the extra blankets and Motrin we can handle in here now."

Slipping into my dinged old green Camry, I decided to poke the elephant in the room on that note.

"Speaking of women," I said casually.

"Nope. I ain't heard shit from her or this supposed lawyer of hers."

Ryan's part-time tweaker wife had left him two weeks before he went to rehab, threatening to have the court keep the kids from him by using the dope in his system as a weapon to prove him unfit—a ploy she had supposedly gotten from some TV lawyer that she had supposedly had at least one of those supposedly free consultations with. She skipped town the Friday after Ryan checked in with an ex-friend of Ryan's, Rodriguez—a soldier from another unit that she'd cheated on him with during our first tour in Iraq.

"She probably took my fucking kids off to Mexico or some shit. They're probably both shooting meth up in their eyeballs in a two room suite at some rundown motel outside of Laredo while both our kids watch Elmo in the other room with a bunch of pervert truckers peeking through the bullet holes in the walls—but fuck it man, life's life. I try not to think about it too much—let's talk about something else."

I searched my throbbing brain from a way to lighten the mood, "Isn't everything else life too, though, grasshopper?" I asked, trying to be funny. Ryan wasn't impressed.

"Comedy's not your strong suit, Tinker Bell. Stick to poetry or whatever hippie shit you college boys are in to these days down in Austin. Anyway, did you hear about Cornell's big promotion?" he asked.

"Yeah, I saw it on Facebook last night. There was a big party at some downtown hotel. It was nice. His wife posted a bunch of pictures--how'd you hear about that?"

"Facebook, motherfucker. We're in rehab, not prison."

"Sorry. I didn't know you had computers."

"Yeah, it ain't lockup. But how about that little Private First Class Cornell all grown up and fancy and shit—who'da thunk it, huh? I loved that banner, 'The Best Vets Helping Vets Get Better.' Anyway, I gotta run. It's time for afternoon group, where we 'Discuss and foster the insight we learned and growth we've made during our deep, soul-searching breakaway time.'"

"What are you going to tell them?"

"That at least we're not in fucking prison yet."

"Or back in the Army, brother."

He never did end up in prison. Or back in the Army. And when he graduated from the rigorous fourteen step healing process that is the New York State St. Christopher at the Adirondacks Wellness and Rehabilitation Center the following spring, he was voted, "least-likely to relapse" and, "most-likely to succeed," nearly unanimously by all the other patients and the nursing staff, which gave us hope.

I drove the long way off campus and stopped to watch the ROTC cadets drilling back and forth across the muddy parade field in their rain gear, with their rubber guns, eager to graduate.

THE MOUNTAIN
By Andrew E. Szala

T he mountain is tall. Late summer leaves. Initially, he pulls his car up. He does not notice anyone at the trailhead. He ventures deeper. He encounters cars, one, two at most. He's unfazed and knows what he is doing. No moment of hesitation, no last glance at his car, the door closes and there is only forward now. He's used to this. The mountain hides the exertion required to proceed.

On his exit from active duty there had been parties. Friends came out of the woodwork at his homecoming, patting him on the back and telling him how they would have joined also but… there was always a but, and a reason why they couldn't put their lives on hold. As the days passed and turned to weeks the friends came by less. While he'd been away they'd gotten on with their lives, and in his mind he had become like a scar, present but not thought of until looked directly at. He and his wife began to fight more. His temper would rage and quickly reach a crescendo before falling abruptly off with his exhaustion. Always exhaustion. Sleep came in sprints and his mind took him back to the desert while he dreamed.

The mountain at its base is wide and the path hot. The trees hold the mountain's breath beneath their leaves. As he passes the de-

scending hikers, only a quick nod is exchanged. His presence
barely registered. How different they seem. His climb is not for
sport, nor fitness. He drinks no water.

He'd felt trapped in his body. Isolated in his mind. His new
sobriety added to his seclusion as he watched those around him
in merriment while he sipped diet coke. Confirming what he already knew; he was different. It was not his presence, but lack
thereof which burned her the most. He was a zombie.

"What's wrong?' became a daily question which he yearned
to answer.

The last hikers pass on the way down. He's alone. The mountain is indifferent. Each step draws him to the peak. He hears no
birds or song.

The necessity of the military, in some capacity, was not up for
debate. He knew this, and while we had made great strides towards peace, our kind will never exist without the presence of evil
draped in the robes of good. He struggled for a long time. Unable
to place into words why it was ok to do the things he had. What
took him the longest to overcome was the fact there was evil on
both sides of any war and like all things, the sum lived in the
grey. His actions held him in high esteem among his peers, but
knowledge muddied this fact.

He would try. He would resolve to be better, to immerse himself in the world and live. But, to fall. He would see around him
the emptiness of a world without the hierarchy of the military.
The outside world had no form and rules were seen as disposable.
It made no sense; who won and lost. He began to build resent-
ment to his own helplessness. He struggled to maintain the bearing the military had built into him. His footholds disappeared.

He entered college in an attempt to better this. He joined
the military for the same reason. Here, he saw it: a tattered yellow ribbon informing all how much the troops would be sup-
ported. After a while all those ribbons began to feel like a lie, a
placebo, made to make their owners feel better about their own
helplessness in a burning world. In the end, no one had to ac-

tually support the troops as long as they said they did. Finding employment reinforced this conclusion. A veteran preference, as a concept, was not readily applied during the hiring process; his skills did not translate.

His time was passing. Sitting in the VA. No one from his war, his guilt at feeling this mattered somehow. Each one seemed somehow different and the same. Was he one of these? So many broken. He was like a child in a physician's office waiting for his grandmother. Some tried, most did not. Their battle was apathy.

When she left he couldn't blame her. When she took his children, what could he say? His mind was absent, his body a shade. He sat, sometimes for days in his world, scrolling through social media, angered by the nature of others' daily problems. They would never know real stress; they would never know real.

When he saw pictures of his wife and her new…that…holding his child it confirmed what he already knew: he did not exist. He had been erased and his story retold without him. Their happiness was a new pain.

He is in the violet world: making his way through the trees, as the path grows hard to see and the journey more beat. His mouth dry, clothes drowned. It was here he saw it, his way out, a small break ahead to take in open air. The mountain's last light.

He felt the forgotten. Used and tossed aside. Disposable for a purpose, a bargaining chip, an advertisement, a discount at a diner where no one wants to eat. One day a year for him and weekend in the spring for his friends past. His anger and guilt at these thoughts came in equal spades. His mind often turned to his brothers who'd passed. He thought of each individual soldier and how they lived. They were not sports stars. They were not beautiful creatures. They were men and women, their blood red. He remembered Abdul, "Aziz," his interpreter, medevac'd after walking over an old mine. He never knew if he survived. Often with combat no closure could be found.

He emerges from the tree line into the sun. Up here he can see the basket of the earth in the valley below. He can see it is larger than him and knows it will exist without him. There before him is a warm expanse of grass and dirt, the soldiers' throne. It only takes a finger.

LIGHTS OUT
by Vance Voyles

T he man squats low against the wall as the patrol car passes in the road behind him. Headlights grow long shadows of parked cars and tree trunks into the space where he sits hidden behind a dumpster. The stench of rotten banana peels, dead milk cartons, and day old diapers surrounds him. He had been expecting more of a response and he smiles at his good fortune. He waits for the engine to turn off and the slam of a car door before he steals a glance to see who they have sent to take him. He shakes his arms to loosen up and rolls his neck. This is what they trained him for. This was who he is now. Rock and roll.

When I first got the call, the dispatcher said witnesses heard screaming and the sounds of breaking glass in the apartment below just before things went quiet. The address had no history of domestic violence. All they wanted was a check on well-being, but as I turn into the complex, the shadow of a big man sprints across the street near the dumpster where the tree-line fills up the space between the highway and the apartments. I reach down and grab the hand mic to the radio and wait for a break in traffic.

"County, 120-Alpha going 97," I say. "Looks like a verbal, can I get a 44?"

"Copy, 120-Alpha," she says. A chatter of radio traffic follows and two more units respond to head in my direction.

Watching the dumpster, I pull into a faded blue handicapped parking spot and turn off the engine. Then, in one swift move, I open the door, grab the heavy flashlight from its charger under the driver's seat, and step out into the night. Other than the slight breeze rustling the trees, there is no movement from the dumpster or anywhere else. Three seconds. Five. I shut the driver's door and move towards the apartments.

Shards of glass sparkle in the breezeway under my flashlight's beam. From the smell of fresh phosphorous, someone has recently smashed the light bulbs dotting the dark corridor. Before knocking, I stand silent with my ear to the door listening for some noise. Anything. After three hard knocks, a girl rips open the door crying, but when she sees me standing there in uniform, with a gun on my hip and a star on my chest, she jumps back and wilts. Her eyes are puffy and she holds a tissue in front of her mouth.

"Is everything okay in there?" I peer behind her to see if anyone else is inside.

"No, I mean, everything's okay now." She holds her arm straight against the door to hold it open. "He took off when I said I was calling the cops."

"Who is he?"

"Jason. My fiancé."

"You mind if we talk inside, Miss?"

"Erin."

"Erin," I repeat. She nods and planks herself against the door to make room for me to pass. "After you," I say, motioning her inside. "You think he'll be back soon?" I take one last look down the breezeway, and follow her into the apartment.

"Who knows?" The hallway into the apartment stands dark in contrast to the living room and kitchen where every light is burning bright. Erin heads straight for the couch, exhausted but wary. She is sitting in the eye of a relationship hurricane, while somewhere outside, storm bands are gearing up for another run at her. "He hasn't been the same since he got back. One minute, he's a sweetheart and the next thing, he's punching lights out with his bare hands. He won't talk about it, and I never know what's going on in his head."

Next to the couch, near the sliding glass door, a black, metal shotgun leans heavy against the wall. I cross the living room to close the gap. "Is this loaded?"

"It's his. So, yes. Probably."

"You mind?" Not waiting for an answer, I pick it up and pull back the slide. One in the chamber and at least one more ready to go. Erin ignores me as I cup the ejection port and unload the shotgun.

She folds her arms against her chest and stares at the ground.

"What did you mean when you said, 'since he came back?' Is Jason in the military?"

"Marines," she says, "but not anymore."

Once the door shuts on his apartment, Jason moves from his position of cover and jogs over to the patrol car. He cups his hand against the glass. Remington shotgun locked in between the driver and passenger seat. Low light streams into the cab from the folded down screen of the laptop computer mounted to the center console. Taking the distance from the dumpster to the squad car, Jason estimates the deputy to be around six-foot, two thirty. Smaller than he is. No pictures on the dash. Nothing to show who the guy is. He moves to the back window. Stickers placed on the cage; Superman, Punisher, The Incredible Hulk, and then the one he is looking for, Tapout.

"All the better," he mutters. "A challenge." Jason clenches his teeth together. Why doesn't she understand what he is doing? They didn't need the police to protect and serve. That was what he is there for. He rubs the sides of his head and balls his hands into fists. The streetlights flood the parking lot and angry bees buzz inside his head. He is losing his night vision. A car door slams. Someone laughs. He needs to move. Get cover. Jason looks around, to his apartment, the bushes, the dumpster, the stairwell.

"So, he's fine one minute, nervous the next, would you say that's right?" I ask.

Erin nods.

"Would you say this happens more at night or during the day?" I jot down her answers in a small pocket notebook. This address needs hazards in the computer for future deputies coming to this apartment.

"I don't know. I mean, I never thought about it like that. When he first got back, it only happened when he drank too much, so I chalked it up to that, you know? Blowing off steam. But then it started happening more and more, over nothing. Like tonight." Erin's eyes are dry now. Clear. Not like they were when she first opened the door.

"What happened tonight?"

She shrugs in confusion. "He ran a red light. Like, for nothing. We were sitting there waiting for it to change. I think I was talking about us moving closer to my parent's house, or something else completely benign, and then he starts tapping the steering wheel and looking back and forth for cars. So, I'm like, 'honey, what's wrong?' and all of a sudden he's in full freak-out mode. 'This fucking light. What the fuck? This fucking light.' And by now, he's banging on the steering wheel. 'What the fuck? What the fuck?' And then he's squealing the tires through the light. I mean, thank God no one was coming." Erin's hands work furiously in front of her telling the story in tandem. "You see what I mean? One minute fine, the next minute, bat-shit crazy."

"Was he drinking tonight?" I ask, regretting it instantly.

"You're not listening. This isn't about him drinking. Sure, we had some beers with dinner, but this shit is happening all the time!" Erin shoulders collapse and she starts crying again. "I love him so much, but what the fuck am I supposed to do?"

I want to reach out to her, rest a hand on her shoulder, and tell her it is all going to be okay. Even if that is a lie. Better yet, I want to send her to some border town in Iraq or Afghanistan and make her walk point to show her what the rest of the world is drowning out with Facebook and Twitter. I want to show her what she is missing. Jason. Both versions of him. The man he used to be and the one he is afraid to tell her about.

But I have a job to do.

"And you said he never hit you, right? At least not tonight?"

Erin slumped back on the couch. "No," she says. "Not yet." At least she has that going for her, knowledge of the possibility.

"I'm going to go outside and see if I can find him. Are there any other guns in the house, besides that one?" I point at the unloaded shotgun. "Or on him, for that matter?"

"No," she says.

I pick up the shotgun on my way out, tuck it under the crook of my left arm, and pocket the rounds in my shirt pocket. "I'm going to go ahead and take this with me for safe keeping. He'll be able to get it back tomorrow."

"He's not going to be happy about that."

"Oh, I'm sure he'll be pissed. But like I said, it's only temporary, just until we can figure out what is going on with him tonight, okay?"

Erin nods, resigned to the reality of her situation.

"And I'm going to get you started on a statement, just to document tonight and his state of mind."

"Are you going to help me at all, or just write stuff down?"

I want to shake her awake. Tell her that this is bigger than her relationship with Jason. That without the proper help, her boyfriend is a time bomb ready to explode. Instead, I smile sympathetically at her.

"I'm going to try to help, but writing it all down is how I get the ball rolling."

White dots blink in my eyes as I step outside the door of Erin's apartment. The sound of distant traffic hums in the distance. He's got to be close by, and it's only crazy if it doesn't work.

"Jason?" I call out into the dark. "Can you hear me?" Nothing. I reach up and rub the crazy, built up adrenaline out of my neck and move towards my car in the parking lot where my back up should be pulling in.

"Looks like you got something that don't belong to you, boot," Jason says from the breezeway behind me. I turn to see him. His eyes light up. His fists are mini-anvils at his sides. "Oh, yeah," he says, his jaw set in stone, breathing heavy through his nose. "Rookie mistake if I ever saw one."

"Hold on a second, brother," I tell him. "We're on the same side."

Jason laughs and a stream of saliva falls from his mouth. "You're not my fucking brother." He almost whispers. "And I don't know what side you're talking about." His chest rises and falls, oblivious to the two deputies who have stepped into the breezeway behind him, my brothers, who have him in handcuffs before he knows what has happened.

Perhaps he got lost in the sound of buzzing in his ears or the pixies of streetlights flitting around his head when he remembered the shotgun heavy in his hands, so cold, even though he knows the warmth of fire from long days of fighting, or how he beat back the dust of a thousand sandstorms as vehicles and buddies broke down or got blown to bits right in front of his eyes. All for the promise of a lie; Erin's faithful understanding. Perhaps everything became clear for him. The enemy is everywhere, and nowhere, and in all parts in between.

As I guide him into the back seat of my patrol car, his hands cuffed behind his back, Jason's eyes turned into glass. The radio squawks, and I tell dispatch I'm heading to Lakeside Alternatives. The doctors can help him better than I can. Then Jason mumbles under his breath from the back seat.

"No." I tell him. "Even if you hadn't come back tonight, we were going to come looking for you. You need help, man." I gesture to the other deputies driving away. "We just want to help."

"You don't get it," Jason says as he flops his head towards the window and the amber glow of streetlights. "The stars are all gone. I should've never come back."

TWO ROADS

by Natalie Lovejoy

To get from Nashville to Baltimore you take I-40 East to I-81 North, cutting through Virginia. Then you take the 495 loop around the clusterfuck that is Washington D.C., which will spit you out on I-95 North to Baltimore. I knew because I had made the drive alone, back and forth, last Christmas while my husband was deployed in Iraq. Now he is at the wheel, and I am in the passenger seat. We are on our way to visit our parents in Maryland before hopping back on I-95 North to go to New York City where I am slated to start grad school in a month, and he is slated to start hunting for a civilian job. It is somehow much less fun this time.

I first visited New York when I was seven years old and afterward declared to my parents that one day I would live there. As I got older and took more trips to the city, this conviction only grew stronger. New York is where those who don't fit in fit in; where a competitive spirit is celebrated, where originality is valued, where high aspirations are the standard, and where every other corner is famous for something. Yes, I was also aware that it was over-priced, over-crowded, old, and sometimes hostile, but none of that mattered to me because I knew home isn't so much a place you go to as it is a place where you belong.

The GPS says it's only thirty-four miles until the beltway. We are sitting in one of our car-trip formations: His eyes locked forward, his back soldier-straight, his jaw tight, his right hand gripping the steering wheel instead of my hand. I sit cross-legged, with my body and eyes tilted toward the passenger window. I imagine the scenery flying by to the beat of the music on the radio and make up stories in my head to go with the songs, as I've done on every car trip since I was about four. I prefer the formation where I sit facing forward and he holds my hand, or the one where I hug his right arm with both of mine while his hand rests on my left thigh, every now and then creeping up my leg until I slap it away, pretending to be offended because I am a lady. Because those formations mean things are good. The way we are sitting now is how we sit when there is something going on that neither of us wants to talk about. I finally go for it.

"Are you upset about something?" I hope he doesn't say what I think he's going to say.

"I'm just nervous. I don't know that this was such a good idea."

That's what I thought he was going to say. I decide to play dumb.

"Do you think we shouldn't've stopped in Bristol?"

"What? No, that's not what I mean."

I know what he means. He's talking about leaving the Army and moving to New York.

All during my grad school application process, he had been encouraging. When I got into NYU, he was thrilled for me.

"Go there, baby. You have to. It's New York! You wanted to go back to New York, and now's your chance! Plus it's the best school for you."

"But it's the most expensive, and New York is expensive. I got into Belmont, too. If I went there, you could stay in at Ft. Campbell and – "

"No, NYU is better for you. Don't pass this up."

With his blessing, I paid my tuition deposit, and set the wheels in motion to go to NYU.

I did it all wrong.

"But you told me to go to NYU! Remember?" I retort, turning down Pete Seeger on the radio.

"Yeah, but that's only because I thought I wasn't coming back."

We wordlessly fall back into formation, and he turns Pete Seeger back up. His reason for encouraging me to go to New York suddenly occurs to me: he entertained this morbid fantasy of heroically dying in battle and leaving me his life insurance, which I would then use to go off to the Big Apple. Instead, he is very much alive, and we are going to one of the most expensive cities in the country, with no jobs lined up, so I can attend one of the most expensive schools in the country in the worst economic crisis with since the Great Depression. Oops.

At our farewell party I had watched the look of panic and judgement cross everyone's face when we told them about our next steps. No, we didn't have jobs yet, but we'd find something. When I had moved to New York four years ago, before my newly-commissioned boyfriend had proposed, I had found a full-time job in less than a month, so I wasn't worried. He wanted to work for the government in some capacity, and as a former Army officer they'd grab him right up. However once the words left my mouth I realized I sounded at best like a trainwreck waiting to happen and at worst like a horrible person who was taking advantage of her sweet soldier's devotion. But there was another problem with our plan that I wouldn't comprehend until a few years down the road. He had returned from Iraq in mid-April. It was now mid-July. Three months. Three months. We hadn't even passed the honeymoon phase yet. Why hadn't anyone told me that asking a veteran to move from the insulation of an Army base to the concrete isolation of New York - after a year in a war-zone, in such short-time span - was a terrible idea for reasons that had nothing to do with me?

I continue to stare out the window and try to feel as nervous as he does, but I can't. I feel guilty for being so excited about our move, but this is the first time in four years that I am something other than a bookmark in someone else's story.

When I first left my job, family, and friends to join my new husband in Ft. Bliss, the intoxicating buzz of newly-weddedness quickly faded into a pounding hangover. My soldier came home to find me sobbing in the middle of our living room floor on a regular basis.

"It seems like you're not happy." He had always been very perceptive.

"I think I'm depressed."

"Why don't you go shopping," he suggested, trying to help. "Or get a manicure?"

Outside the car it starts to drizzle, and my mind drifts to the deployment a year later. By then I'd learned to keep my outbursts to myself – in fact, it was my patriotic duty to do so. Don't tell him about your problems because it will upset him, and he needs to focus on the mission. It's ok for you to be upset but not for him to be. Because what he's doing is important and what you're doing is not. Because his life is important and yours is not. At least not as important as his. This is your role in life, and you must accept it. You need to accept not mattering as much. But it's really not so bad – you get a roof over your head, free dental cleanings, and tax-free shopping at the PX. Mattering is overrated. Calm down, woman, and treat yourself to a manicure.

I'm over-reacting and over-analyzing as usual, my husband would tell me; my husband who doesn't talk much, who never cries, who makes both his pain and joy invisible, who doesn't need me. No wonder the Army loved him. Meanwhile, it had become apparent that I had the completely wrong disposition to be a military wife. A military wife is supposed to be there to encourage, not challenge; to enhance his life, not have her own. I mean, not unless it's to have a portable career as a medical billing specialist.

But after awhile my soldier seemed to be growing disillusioned as well.

"Once I'm done with this deployment, I'm definitely going to be looking to get out of the military," he had told me during one static-y phone conversation.

"It's complicated to explain," he went on. "But I'm tired of dealing with Army BS. I'm not sure what I'm going to be doing as soon as I get out, but I'll be looking for a job while I'm over here. I know there are plenty of things I can do. The possibilities are really endless!"

We finally approach the outskirts of D.C., and he takes the ramp for 295.

"You should take 495. There's less traffic," I say, even though I know it's too late.

"No, there's more traffic on 495 at this time of day."

"No, there's more traffic on 295."

"I used to live here."

"So did I!"

"Just let me fucking drive!"

The car goes silent again, and we again resume our formation — the bad one. I stare out the passenger window in a way I hope conveys I'm mad enough to jump out of it. And I could, too, because the car comes to a complete stop due to the wall of commuters ahead of us. He slams on the brakes just in time and grinds his teeth in defeat, and I'm both smart and dumb enough to keep staring out the window as if we're still speeding along at seventy-five miles an hour.

Because to be honest, I don't yet know which road is best because I have no idea where we're headed. I don't know yet how he will resent me for finding employment within the first week of our move while he can't even find the ambition to leave our apartment. I don't know yet how I will resent him for spending the next six months listlessly poking around the internet for job openings while I work from 10am-4pm and go to class from 5pm-9pm, commuting an hour each way, only to come home to the dishes from breakfast still sitting in the sink, the bed unmade, and the refrigerator empty save for some beers and leftover Chinese food. I don't yet know government jobs have a year-long waiting list. I don't yet know that even GameStop at the Jersey City Mall won't hire him.

I don't yet know that he won't be able to just "get over it."

I don't yet know that the only people who will make him feel accepted are the other members of his reserve unit, and that they will keep us afloat by giving him temporary assignments for the following six months. And I definitely don't know yet that after a year of unemployment he will re-enlist with the Army for good, B.S. and all, and that three years later we will be divorced. But really, how could I expect my Army veteran husband – military brat and brother of a marine, son of a marine (who was also the son of a marine), brother-in-law of an airman, and nephew of two Navy men – to fit in anywhere else?

He finally takes my hand. I look at him. He smiles at me cautiously, and I return it, cautiously.

"I'm sorry I yelled. I still love you."

"It's ok. I love you, too," I say quickly.

"I'm sure everything's going to be fine. We love each other, and that's the important thing. Everything else will work itself out." He squeezes my hand, and I squeeze his hand back. "And look," he continues, "The traffic is clearing up. We'll probably be home in time for dinner."

And that is true. We are both headed home.

BETCHA.I.CAN

by Gail Chatfield

don't remember his name but I will never forget the email address he left on the sign in sheet: betcha.i.can@gmail.com

Such a positive, uplifting username for someone whose life was obviously in the midst of a downward descent.

Betcha.i.can came to one of our Veterans' Writing Group meetings a while back. It wasn't exactly what he had planned to do that morning when he walked into the Community Room. Back then, we met right next to the Police Department in Oceanside which, for some unknown economic reason, was closed on Saturdays and provided an interesting mix of people wandering in our doors.

Betcha.i.can looked about 24 or 25 years old as he stood in the doorway asking for spare change to use the pay phone right outside. In a rapid-fire explosion of words he told me that he didn't have a cell phone and really needed to call his friend because he had no place to stay and his other friend's wife or maybe it was a girlfriend had kicked him out. His voice rose in volume as he described the places he had stayed and the shit (his word) that happened to him over the last couple of months. He finished his chronicle saying things were really just fucked up.

Obviously, plus you are high on something, I thought to myself.

He was hurting and I was, I admit, fearfully uncomfortable. Looking back I regret that I judged him on his appearance and his choice of vignettes to share. But there he was, meth-infused eyes, cropped blond hair, muscled, tattooed arms exposed by a wife beater t-shirt and worst of all, he blocked my only means of escape. Then in a literal blink of his eyes and a panic beat of my heart, he asked in a relatively calm voice what we were doing in the room.

I said it was the Veterans Writing Group meeting and we would start soon.

"I like to write. Is it free? Do you have to join?" he said again with that rat-a-tat-tat delivery.

"Yes it's free, you just have to be a vet," I answered, wishing the rest of the group would arrive soon.

Betcha.i.can said he didn't have his DD214 with him. He just got out of the Navy and all his stuff is at his dad's in Fallbrook and he can't go back there because he is not speaking to his dad ever again, something about stuff in the attic, things being stolen, and some motherfucker all up in his face. He wasn't making much sense but only a vet would use the term DD214 so I told him that we didn't need to see his discharge papers and he's welcome to stay.

"Yeah, and I have all these notebooks." And with that he bolted out of the room.

The group arrived and we began our meeting. I truly thought the young man probably forgot about coming back.

But a few minutes later, in walked betcha.i.can wearing a clean short-sleeved shirt over his wife beater and carrying a stack of notebooks. I was thankful for that gesture. To me, putting on a shirt meant he still had some dignity and pride despite his troubled and erratic demeanor. He had hope.

Our mentor from the Writers Guild Foundation encouraged lots of discussion but betcha.i.can just couldn't settle down. He kept wiggling in his seat and saying random comments to those around him. He sat in the only squeaky chair in the room and made quite a racket when his notebooks fell and he struggled to pick them up.

The mother in me was concerned about his well-being, but I also wanted to shout a very unmotherly, "Shut the fuck up and stop squirming around." But I didn't. His mumbling and jittering continued to distract but the guys next to him showed great tolerance and patience.

The mentor then asked if anyone had something they would like to read. Betcha.i.can's hand shot up.

This should be interesting, I thought.

But what this young man couldn't convey lucidly with his spoken words, he could with his written ones. He read one short story using a butterfly as a metaphor for his sister whom he obviously loved and felt he needed to protect. And then completely changing emotional directions, he shared a story about being beat up by some guys who were his friends. Naturally, a woman and alcohol were involved, and he ended up with a bleeding gash on his head. When it was all over, he felt no anger towards his friends. "They did what they had to do," he said reading the last line.

His stories were raw and unpolished but they were also passionate and insightful. I held back tears as he read some passages, laughed at others. Betcha.i.can's writing style impressed our mentor who urged him to keep writing and transfer his stories to a computer since some of his notebooks had already been lost, stolen, or left behind in places he stayed.

I wanted to reach out and hug that wounded little boy and tell him everything would be alright. He was wrestling in a troubled sea and mothers can be good lifeguards. I wondered where his own mother was and why she was not taking better care of her son. But families are complicated, and he is a grown man after all. I wanted to help. Naively, I thought he might listen to my motherly tough-love advice and wisdom. Yeah, right, my own daughter was going through a difficult time and she wasn't listening to me.

For the rest of the meeting, I practiced in my mind how I

would connect with him after the class.

Here was my plan: I'd corner him, block his exit and have him tremble with fear from this mother-talker all up in his face. I'd be like Cher in the movie Moonstruck when she slapped Nicholas Cage's face and said, "Snap out of it." But he was probably two years old when that movie came out so I doubt he would understand or appreciate my reenactment.

And this is what I would tell him:

Do you know how lucky you are to be 20-something years old? You have all of life's wonder, opportunities and possibilities ahead of you. Use the GI Bill and get an education. If you're hurting, seek help. Know that so many people are dedicated to making sure you are healthy, happy and whole. I don't know what you did in the Navy but you had adventures, experiences and gained a world view of life few of your generation have. You have stories to tell. You will no doubt be the most interesting person in a roomful of your civilian peers. I know, I have a daughter your age, and trust me, some of her guy friends are not all that interesting. Do something with your life before you become a cliché or worse, a statistic. You are good looking but spend too much time tweaking and you will lose that nice complexion and those white teeth will rot out. That muscle mass holding up those tats will soon shrivel and that skin canvas of beautiful, painful artwork will melt together like crayons left out in the sun."

When class was over, I did get right into his face but I froze. I was only able to say the lamest phrase ever: "Stop taking drugs and do something with your life." Some mother I am.

Even as he mumbled, "Yeah I know," he knew, I knew, he didn't know. And then he walked away. I can't really blame him for blowing me off. I'm sure to him I was just some middle-aged woman about to drone on and kill his buzz. Hell, my own generation didn't trust anyone over 30.

In the end, we gave betcha.i.can the rest of the pretzels and a few bottles of water and left him standing there outside the Community Room with his backpack in a shopping cart waiting for some friend to pick him up. My last words to him were, "You are a good man, take care of yourself and do great things." Sounds really lame now as I write those words.

I wished we could have done more, perhaps took him to Interfaith Shelter or a homeless facility. But we never thought to have that information handy. We do now, just in case.

My partner in the writing group, John, a retired Marine, is such a good guy that every time he drove down Mission Blvd, he looked to see if he could find him and offer help. Leave no man behind. John didn't have any luck.

I think about that young sailor from time to time with a heavy heart.

Is he disheveled and disillusioned, getting high in the back streets of Oceanside?

Or maybe he's sitting in a classroom at Mira Costa College or Cal State San Marcos writing his stories. Perhaps he leans over and slips this cute, smart girl sitting next to him his email address: betcha.i.can@gmail.com.

THREADS OF FICTION
by Andrew Miller

n camo uniform and boots, travel-stained, I had a blurry walk
through an American airport. I was home from ten months in
Afghanistan for R&R. In about 96 hours, I was ordering spicy
chicken sandwiches instead of artillery strikes. I was a first lieutenant, an artillery officer attached to an infantry unit.

This airport was the first stop after Kuwait, preceded by Afghanistan's Bagram air base. Post-Ambien, forced into wakeful-
ness to move forward, as anyone who travels with the military
knows; I was aware of little except the need to push on. A woman hugged me, people clapped at me, I was surrounded. I was a
soldier visiting home, but these people wanted my time. They
wanted to know that I knew they cared. I knew they were loud,
they were between me and my flight onward to Chicago, and
they were touching me. A woman handed me a stuffed bear; I
placed it in the trash. I saw my mother in Chicago.

* * *

One day a man wrote to me to express his thanks. We both
participated in a writing group for veterans, and he had borrowed
a line of mine for his poetry. I had written it in reflection of that
first airport ambush:

The return from war should be a solemn experience.

That poet was one of the first to tell me about his generation's terrible return from war. In contrast, I knew my cheering crowds and flag-waving experiences seemed benign. Still, I suspected cynical motivations. Perhaps even guilt-driven knee-jerk celebrations to forget what those other veterans endured. I have mixed feelings on comparing experiences with other veterans. When you come home with your stories, you've got to be the harshest critic of your own work. Nobody else will dare criticize you, so it's double duty. I expect the same of any other veteran; it's already hard enough to make civilians care about war when you're telling the truth. That sounds like a contradiction, but let me explain: when I say "care about war," I mean critically, as in, consider wars in the context of everyone's best interest. Showering soldiers with feel-good moments is not an act of care with respect to war. It may hurt less than shunning draftees of dubious conflicts, but I judge it as wasted energy.

* * *

My very first creative nonfiction work was awful writing in journals about loneliness and being afraid to talk to girls. I've never thrown those journals out, so a part of me sensed their value. I aged through adolescence and life got more confusing rather than less, and I stopped writing.

I felt trapped by the suggestions and needs of others. I never allowed myself time to think on my own, for what I wanted out of life. In that regard, my early adulthood was typical. My eventual response, joining the army, perhaps less so. I came from privilege: an upbringing in a Chicago suburb known for McMansions and well-funded public schools. The fiction I lived by put me in the mindset to join the army. I had minor family history, a desire to kick the can on "serious" life decisions like a career path, and the lucrative scholarships and padding that military service contributes to a resume.

They told me college was where I belonged after high school, that I was smart. They told me military service was honorable and respectable. I couldn't imagine doing anything other than gaining approval, and so the world I knew in high school liked that I accepted my ROTC scholarship.

"This will benefit me later," I told myself. My heart was not in it, but I showed up daily and did my work. I never fit in. I always knew, but never allowed myself to consider, that the answers I wanted would come without effort. I wanted that fiction so badly: to show up, wear a uniform, and be different. Better.

Soon, after six years of active duty and two combat deployments to Afghanistan, I was a civilian again. I tried writing again, and linked up with a veterans writing group at Syracuse University. I got to know another writer - a memoirist and a green beret medic who served in Vietnam and was wounded in combat. He had suffered his own post-war Odyssey trying to find happiness in bottles, business ventures and divorces. He waited 30 years to get help from the VA. While we spoke, he never said a word about the man he was looking at. I knew what he thought. I went to the VA shortly afterwards.

* * *

At the 2013 Veterans Day parade in Syracuse, New York, there were hunched WWII veterans with yellow and red insignias and patches on their caps and vests. They were saluting me. I was riding at the front of a local Veterans Day Parade in a classic WWII-style jeep with a big sign on the front: Grand Marshal Andrew Miller. The veterans were cheering for me and the other grand marshal, an Iraq War veteran. We were part of the "30 Heroes Under 30" contest sponsored by a local New York state assemblyman. Some colleagues at my workplace had nominated me. I knew I stood out: I was an artillery officer, not a grunt. There were young and old veterans in the contest and at the parade who looked at me in the jeep, and I wondered why our positions weren't reversed. I didn't have their awards for combat bravery or battle wounds. Once again, I had acquiesced to the suggestions of others. It was too late to back out.

The crowds were thick and bundled against the cold November air. After the jeep ride, I stood on a stage with the other grand marshal and waved at the floats. I didn't deserve the 15 minutes of fame and I was up there as the poster boy for a pampered generation that fought a war nobody cared about until it was time to clap. Sometimes I believe it, sometimes I don't, but on that stage all I could think about were the Vietnam, Korea and WWII vets who had this "hero" jammed in their faces. Maybe they cared about my war, but I wasn't ready for their respect.

I wanted to see the civilians stop clapping. If they understood any of it, there wouldn't be a single cheer. They'd stand silent, thankful for the pain of the cold to complement what hurt the most: they were surrounded by us, veterans, survivors, who gathered on that holiday because we missed our friends. Why had I agreed to any of this? The crowds felt obligated to the veterans, who I can't speak for, but I felt obligated to the crowds. I had made my own decision to join; I wasn't drafted to serve my country. I got a scholarship out of it. While serving, I saw life distilled down to its best and worst: life-saving trust and mortal violations. None of those things felt appropriately served by a parade or celebration. This Veterans Day circus in particular felt like an excess of misunderstanding and back-patting.

That was my final act of fiction. I still keep that big white sign around, the one with my name in red and blue letters. I like to tell people what it means, with the hope they'll seek a more critical understanding of the good and bad that comes with war. I hope they'll help me search for narratives in which veterans retain control.

I'll say it again: the return from war should be a solemn experience.

EPILOGUE FOR WAR CORRESPONDENCE
By Nathan Webster

Veterans can mock their war, if they want. They can exaggerate it, glorify it, try to forget it, but once a boot goes in the sand, it's theirs for good.

I know the feeling; before arriving in Iraq as a journalist, I had gone as a soldier during Desert Storm. I've talked that up and I've played it down. In the end, my war reduced itself to a framed trophy hanging on a wall - a hand-drawn diagram of a MiG fighter cockpit I carved from its original frame in Tallil Air Base in southern Iraq near Nasiriyah, carefully shepherding it back home, through the sand and the heat.

If I took the poster from its glass frame today, I'm certain the dry laminated paper would still smell like the desert, and the desert smelled like tent canvas and boot leather.

The musty perfume that always takes me back.

So, no, a veteran can't ever give their war away; in fact, the day will come when the war takes even something more. A memory, a smell, an image, something once mundane will now trigger the nostalgia.

No trade; the war just grabs and holds. Maybe something big, maybe something small. Something to make a soldier say, "Oh yeah. Like back when I was overseas."

"Overseas." A word to sum it up. Waiting for the planes, getting vaccinations, filling out the paperwork, gathering gear, making last phone calls, departing, landing, laughing, hoping, wishing, wondering, always wondering.

"Overseas," is supposed to gather it all together, and have it make sense for anyone else who ever asks.

On my flight home in 2008, the man next to me wonders where I'm headed from. Kuwait, I tell him, by way of Baghdad.

He asks how it's going there, and I tell him a lot better than the year before. That's good, he says.

"So who pays for you to go?" He asks me.

I don't answer; point my thumb back toward myself.

"Wow. Really? Does it cost a lot?"

Cost? Not much at all, if money's all you're worried about.

I start telling him about the trip, about the soldiers and the heat, but the words sound empty as I explain. I'm trying to tear it all down into some relatable minutia, and I need more time.

Eventually I shrug, and just say, "It went okay."

And I kept waiting, at the end of the second and third trip, for that certain feeling.

Preparing to depart in 2007, the feeling had washed over me at FOB Speicher's airstrip, just outside Tikrit, settled into a C-130 seat bound for Kuwait.

Our flight would leave well after midnight. We had such a puny passenger load they didn't bother having us palletize our luggage and we carried our own duffel bags onto the plane.

We got off the shuttle to the tarmac and our little group headed toward the plane; a long line of soldiers disembarked and walked past, burdened by rucksacks and weapons. In the dark I looked at them and didn't worry if they could see me staring.

On the plane I took my seat. We could stretch out and sleep if we wanted, the plane was now so empty.

We went wheels up 45 minutes, an hour, later.

I felt light as the wheels left the ground, lighter than the plane. I felt a tug on my shoulders, a gravity-defying lightness behind my eyes and in my mind.

I didn't know. So I didn't pay attention.

I didn't know to pay attention as that moment was coming; then it was there, then it was gone.

Later, I reflected. What a funny sensation, but that was all.

In Baghdad, a year later, I boarded another near-empty plane again, back to Kuwait. It was workmanlike, and I fell asleep in moments, woke up on the descent.

Still another year later, I looked at my watch at the moment of flight, at 9:22 p.m. on June 19, 2009, the last time, I was sure, I would ever depart Iraq. This flight was packed and steamy. My glasses fogged, slowly acclimated. I stared in the gloom at a pretty Air Force crewman, a woman sitting in the observation port, elevated with straps above her passengers. But it was all business.

I had departed Iraq after Desert Storm in 1991 with no meaningful moment. Drove south from Iraq into Saudi Arabia one day; never drove back. Flew home from Dhahran in an anticlimactic mob of men and duffel bags.

Not like how I felt in 2007. A feeling I never had before, would never have again.

After returning from that third, 2009 trip, I read a paragraph a soldier had said to me. He had sat on a cot waiting to head home on leave, while I waited to leave for good. He talked about the bad old days.

"When we got to FOB Speicher," he said, "after leaving Bayji for the last time, I got to the chow hall and some girl was there, she wasn't a soldier, was some Red Cross girl, volunteering or something. I don't even know.

"I started to talk to her; I was so happy to see a girl.

"All of a sudden, it just came out of nowhere. I started laughing; couldn't stop. And it got worse. Then tears started pouring down my face. I was still laughing, but now I was crying; got so bad I couldn't even talk.

"She finally just got up and walked away."

He'd been there 15 months, from 2006 to 2007, and would

be there twelve more, from 2008 to 2009.

And now he's nowhere at all, dead in a house fire, back at home. It would make me angry, if there was anyone to be angry at.

The mere month I spent with him at the Bayji JSS didn't earn by any measure the feeling his words finally helped me recognize. But I felt it even so.

I felt light headed, I knew, in that C-130 that night flying out of Speicher, I felt lightheaded because that night of August 2007, I knew I was going to live.

Fingers against an Airbus window, I had traced I-95's southern path, the long runway at Pease airport, the three bridges over the Piscataqua River from New Hampshire into Maine, the cluster of Portsmouth's Market Square; home, 30,000 feet below.

Almost, could I pick out the field behind my house, not far off I-95. I saw, I'm sure, even if I couldn't identify.

The moment answered a question I used to ask myself, standing in the sprawling hayfield of my backyard. Down there below, I had once watched an airplane's lazy, cloudy contrails pass horizon to horizon, ambivalently curious about their origins, traveling the Great Circle trans-continental routes over the North Atlantic.

Where, overseas, can those planes take you and from where do they return?

On August 8, 2007, flying above Stratham, New Hampshire, I tapped on the window with a feeling of homesick relief.

But I might have closed my eyes if I had realized what I'd see the next time I strolled the field and looked up to a jetliner's faint trace of icy mist splitting through all the blue; what I'd really see.

Once I could have wondered; now I would remember.

So many gave their blood and sweat, and then they give a little more.

Smoky snowball trails of hayfield daydreams fade into the sand and to the heat.

Iraq has claimed that memory; Iraq, you took the sky.

PINK CARBON COPIES
by Derrick Woodford

I felt ashamed for crying in basic training, but it was Christmas Day, and when I looked around, the criers were the majority. Grown men longing to be with their families and significant others, but instead, stuck in basic training on Lackland Air Force Base in San Antonio, Texas. There were far worse places we could be, and some of us were likely to see those places with a career in the military, but I wanted to be home. I wanted to be home having a slice of my mother's pecan pie and listen to her sing Motown Christmas carols as she cooked and baked in the kitchen, a complete one-eighty from just a few weeks prior when I couldn't have left Cleveland soon enough.

* * *

I questioned whether or not it was counterproductive to have come out to my mother then join an organization whose policy at the time was don't ask, don't tell. I was eighteen, fresh out of high school, and very naïve about what was socially acceptable at the time. My parents were divorced and had not been on speaking terms for years.

I sat my mother down in the living room, just the two of us. My mouth felt dry and I had the distinct feeling that the words wouldn't come when my lips began to move.

"I'm gay."

She cursed under her breath and just stared at me for a moment. Then came a barrage of what I can only imagine were rhetorical questions and statements, since I wasn't given time to respond.

"Are you sure? Have you been with a woman? I mean a real woman? This can't be happening. Have you prayed on it? You're going to get AIDS. Aren't you afraid of AIDS?"

In retrospect, I would have been equally surprised if she'd been accepting. No more than twenty minutes later we were driving across town to my Aunt Ellen's home. The three of us took the worn staircase to Aunt Ellen's bedroom. We held hands at the foot of the bed, but not before she rubbed olive oil on our foreheads. The olive oil was used to symbolize purity and faith. It would be years later that I learned people actually cook with it, because up to that point, I had only seen it used in prayer.

Aunt Ellen held both our hands and started to pray.

"Yes, Jesus.... ! Thank you, Jesus.... Say 'Thank you, Jesus.' Give him his praise," she commanded.

My mother and I repeated in unison, "Thank you, Jesus."

Like all the times before, Aunt Ellen was soon speaking in tongue and she then broke the circle and laid hands on me.

"Yes, yes ... destruction! You're heading down the path of destruction my son! Don't let the Devil lead you astray! He is a liar, a cheat, and a thief! He's out to kill, steal, and destroy! He wants your soul!" she shouted, with the fiery tone of a preacher. I felt numb. She went on for several more minutes.

I don't know how long we were in the bedroom praying, but when it was all over with, I was drained, confused, and more hopeless than when we started.

Just barely out of high school, I moved out on my own but still spent the next couple of years being assaulted with bible verses and looks of disappointment. Somehow, just living in the same city felt unbearable. I was the proverbial black sheep—an outcast. I decided I needed to leave.

* * *

The enlistment process was a blur. I remember tests and plenty of paperwork. At one point, I was downtown lined up with about thirty other guys. We were all in our underwear being subjected to physicals and exams and herded around. We were barefoot and the floor was cold. Later, there were stacks of paperwork presented to me by my recruiter for signature. Most sheets were white, but occasionally I was presented with a pink or yellow form with carbon copies. One was a health questionnaire. My eyes immediately focused on the black line created by magic marker, in order to conceal a particular question. The exact wording eludes me, but ultimately, it was asking if I was a homosexual. The don't ask don't tell policy was so new that the paperwork hadn't even been changed yet.

* * *

After basic training and technical school, I was enroute to my first duty station—Eielson Air Force Base, the place I would live the next three years. During a layover in Anchorage, I boarded a much smaller plane than the one I'd arrived on, a sign Fairbanks didn't have quite the draw of Anchorage. I couldn't have been more of an oddity on the flight. The average age of the passengers on board was around sixty and I was the only person of color. The flight was less than an hour, just enough time to guzzle down a Dixie cup of Coke and explain to the gray-haired gentlemen sitting beside me that I was reporting to my first duty station. He thanked me for my service.

As I got off the plane, the air was musky, like I'd smelled once before at camp when I was twelve. The counselor said that was the smell of, "fresh air." I followed the crowd into the airport directly from the tarmac we disembarked on, cringing once inside at the stuffed moose, bears, and other wildlife passed off as airport décor.

After checking in at the base, I used a phone in the common area to call my mother. Luckily it was deserted.

"I made it here," I said. "It's different."

"I can't believe you're in Alaska. It's so far away," she said.

"How are you feeling?" I asked.

A couple months before my departure, she was having respiratory issues and was diagnosed with Lupus.

"I'm doing better. God is good," she said.

She also went from part-time saint to full time saint. She no longer wore pants or make-up. She put her hair in a swooped up church lady bun daily.

"I just wanted to check-in. I need to get settled."

"Okay... I'm praying for you."

* * *

We were the cable dogs. We installed and repaired telephone trunk cables, both underground and aerial. Upon my arrival to Eielson, the shop was nearly completing the installation of the Local Area Network to all the buildings on base. They were just getting the Internet. Our shop maintained a workforce of eight to twelve people at a time, depending on the comings and goings.

Most of the guys were married. There was something about Alaska that made people couple-off quickly—even the young ones. At times, we worked hard. Foosball tournaments went on daily during lunch. I was the go-to guy only if a fourth player was needed and no one in a two-mile radius was available. Dipping chewing tobacco was another pastime of theirs, and I was warned to always check my Coke because there was that one time someone took a swig from the wrong can. They compared who had the loudest or smelliest farts, I declined. They hunted and fished in their spare time, I drank and partied. They knew I was different, but I hoped they believed I just wasn't into crazy white people shit, not gay. Either way, they never treated me any worse for it.

* * *

Back then Fairbanks didn't exactly have gay bars and the Internet was barely on the scene. Long before my arrival, I had done my research and that led me to Alaska Land, a thirty-three acre theme park.

The park was designed to look like an authentic gold mining town from the 1920s. I walked by a general store, a life-sized riverboat placed in the center of the park, a carousel, a gazebo, and a modern day food court. It was after-hours, so the park was quite deserted. This could not be the place, I thought, but the gay travel guide I purchased months prior said, "Seek out the Saloon."

It was more of a borrowed space than a gay bar. During the day it was filled with families and tourists visiting the historic park, but at night, you had the likes of me lurking around looking for others like me. The whole situation felt very clandestine and unsettling to me, which gave me the feeling of wrongdoing, like the Gestapo could bust through the door at any moment.

The DJ was set-up near a stage framed by a thick red velvet curtain, where I pictured a line of can-can dancers performing for grungy prospectors. There was the typical moose head hanging on the wall along with mining paraphernalia, and it nearly looked like your average TGI Friday's. A few tables and chairs remained on the floor, while others were pushed aside for what I reasoned was to make room for dancing. No one was dancing.

Incidentally, the people in attendance very much reminded me of prospectors. Thick beards and flannel were the dress code, but nothing like the groomed hipster crowd of today. These were just real Alaskan men, who just happened to be gay, who didn't give a fuck about what was in fashion. They were scary to me. Not intimidating necessarily, but in a "you sort of look homeless please don't touch me," sort of way. I sat in a corner sipping my beer, wondering how I was going to make it through the next few years. I envisioned a future of celibacy, meditating, and lots of exercise.

But on one of my trips to the Saloon I met Damon. He was stationed on Fort Wainwright, just on the edge of town. He was tall, lean, with a mocha complexion. I noticed him early, talking with a couple of girls on the other side of the bar.

"Ah shit, another brotha." he said, and introduced himself.

To reasons even unknown to me, I immediately felt awkward and guarded. I was in Alaska. In the military, I hadn't done the song and dance of meeting someone in quite some time. Often you would meet a guy at the Saloon who claimed to be there for the music, because apparently the Saloon played the best fuckin' music in town, but I figured out his game when he asked if I wanted to dance.

I hesitated and looked around. Only a handful of people bounced around on the dance floor and I felt as if people were already watching us, but before I could say no, he pulled me out onto the floor. Suddenly, I had no rhythm. I did an awkward two-step.

When I'd had enough, I offered to buy us a round of drinks. As I handed him his beer, I noticed the wedding ring.

"Just a marriage of convenience," he smirked.

I didn't know whether or not to believe him. It was a phrase thrown around a lot in private inner circles of military personnel. People married for more money, to get out of the dorms and assignments. At that moment, I don't think I particularly cared.

Over time, the more I got to know Damon the more I sometimes wished we hadn't met. It wasn't that he was a bad person, or hurtful, but he reminded me of myself. The person I was trying to escape. I could have been coerced into marriage and lived a miserable existence, too. I would later find out the wife of convenience he spoke of was fully aware of his sexuality, but was desperately trying to save their marriage with the help of Jesus and the church.

Frankly, his world confused me. One day, sex with me. The next day he's confessing his sins to his pastor at church, where he was deacon. It saddened me that Damon was desperately trying to do right but would always short in the eyes of his faith.

* * *

My time in Alaska felt like a prison sentence at times. There were people in my life, but most, with the exception of Damon, felt like acquaintances. None of them really knew me, because I didn't allow them to. To survive, I had to live under the radar. It was like three years of solitary confinement.

* * *

About three months before my separation, I was on the telephone speaking with my mother when she broached the subject of my separation.

"So after three months, you're done?" she asked. "You can come home?"

I don't know when I made the decision not to return to Cleveland. Over my enlistment, the more time I spent away, the less connected I felt to my place of birth. I landed a job with Homeland Security in 2002 upon my separation from the Air Force and relocated to San Diego.

Shortly after I moved, my brother called while I was on my way to work. His voice was heavy.

"I found her," he said. "She was home alone and I found her this morning."

"What are you talking about?"

"Mom," he said. "She's gone."

I looked around, surrounded by cars, unable to move.

The thought of my mother alone with no one there seemed unfair to me. Living in California, away from home, suddenly felt like a selfish act.

I thought about the last conversation I had with my mom.

"Hey, do you remember that saxophone solo you had in 11th grade?" she asked.

I didn't know why she would bring up something so random and so long ago, but I said that I did.

"I was so proud of you," she said. "And I still am."

She would pass away two days later. I wondered if this was her last gift to me, releasing her firstborn from the torment and confusion she knew I battled with, and maybe indirectly contributed to. I knew, through it all, that she only wanted the best for me. Mistakes were made, but I knew she did her best. Now we were both free.

LAST YEAR
by Anthony Moll

When you jump ship, you either swim for shore or drown.
— Propagandhi

On December 21st, 2009, just shy of eight years after I left home in a hurry to join the U.S. Army, I am in the driver's seat, leaving an Army base in suburban Maryland, wearing my uniform for the last time.

"I know you're not going to miss it," my First Sergeant, a refrigerator of a man in army fatigues, tells me just before I go. "A lot of guys do, but you've got some things going for you." It's one of the last things said to me in uniform, offered just before I step out into the winter air. This is my final commendation from a military leader.

* * *

On December 22nd, 2010, just a year after my last day in the Army, the world's most powerful man pulls back a wooden chair and sits down at a desk on a stage decorated with the flags of each branch of service. The President is in a dark suit. A small American flag pin rests on his lapel. Behind him there is a small crowd of lawmakers also in dark suits, except for the women in bright colors, who huddle in to be seen by the cameras. The chairman of the military's Joint Chiefs of Staff neither smiles nor frowns as he stands in his Navy dress uniform. The Vice President grins his old man grin. The two former service members on stage are at the end of a tour of duty in which they have acted as the face of a law that said those who love members of the same sex were unfit to serve openly in the military.

The President, smiling, signs the paper on the desk, and a bill transforms into law. They call it a repeal. We call it a wrong made right. He signs it with two boxes full of pens, a strange standard applied whenever new laws are signed, and when he is finished, he looks out at the crowd, smiling. He slaps his palm down at the table. "This is done."

* * *

In December 2009, I don't come out of the closet. I should say, I don't come back out of the closet. I was out at sixteen, but the aforementioned law pushed me into eight years of a strange sort of bullshitting; even though many people seemed to assume I was queer, I wasn't allowed to say it. Or to hold hands. Or to go on dates anywhere near the bases where I was stationed. Or to visit the barracks rooms of other queer soldiers without the heart-thudding fear of being burst in on. I don't come back out for two more months, despite being hired by the biggest gay and lesbian nonprofit organization in the country. I'm on separation leave, leave time spent at the end of my contract for the sake of making my last day of work arrive a few weeks earlier. This means that although I'm out of the Army, I'm still, technically, in the Army on paper.

For weeks after I take off the uniform, something keeps me in, keeps me silent. I have yet to escape a sense of duty about the Army, a sense of what I should and shouldn't stand for as a representation of the modern soldier. It's also fear that keeps me in. Irrational fear, really. Fear that I'll lose my veterans benefits. Fear that I'll be pulled back in. Fear related to years of listening to my peers and my bosses talk about how they'd kick a soldier's ass, or worse, if they knew he was gay. I've yet to repair the injury caused by being fearful for years that I would, at best, be asked to leave, that I would be told that I don't belong.

* * *

In December 2010, only a few people in my office know that I date women. I've been seeing the same woman for a few years now, but here in this gay office in D.C., everyone assumes I mean boyfriend or husband when I say "partner."

When I came back out earlier this year, I did so in the most theatrical of ways. (Although it is hard to call it a coming out; No one suspected I was straight at that point.) The day I formally got out of the military, the day the ink dried, the day any real risk in doing so disappeared, gay blogs across the country shared a letter that I wrote to the President, calling for the end of the law called "Don't Ask, Don't Tell." In the letter, I come out as bisexual again, and I brag about my silent service.

To be honest, at this point I identify as pansexual – something akin to bisexual, but rejecting the concept that gender and sex are binary and uniform concepts. Because the letter is a rhetorical act, a marketing ploy aimed at a right-leaning audience, I keep it simple.

Even in my reemergence, I act cautiously, I am limited.

* * *

In December 2009, before I go, I'm not exactly passing for heterosexual. In uniform I am not a towering presence. I have a slight lisp and overly-groomed eyebrows. I often forgo the required beret in my uniform because I don't want to mess up my hair. I don't hide that I've got a gay job lined up in D.C. In this hyper-masculine, heteronormative culture, I stand out.

I'm also the non-commissioned officer assigned to lecture my unit on the regulations regarding sexual harassment, equal opportunity and the current policy restricting open service for gay and lesbian troops in the military. This isn't punishment or an inappropriate joke on the part of my bosses; I volunteered for this position.

The last presentation I gave on these subjects wasn't much different from the rest. A few dozen troops in their uniforms packed into a classroom as I flipped through a slideshow presentation.

"The goal of the Army's Equal Opportunity policy is to ensure fair treatment of all soldiers." I tell them again, the same mandatory message they heard last quarter and the quarter before.

When the part on "Don't Ask, Don't Tell" comes up, I feel the room get quieter. I feel it as a stillness on my skin, as if these warriors were holding their breath. Or not. The truth is, very few soldiers really gave much consideration to the rule. Even in this conservative culture, most of the people who have work to do every day don't seem to care anymore. It's a non-issue nowadays. It is as likely as not that any tension in the air during these sessions was imagined by a soldier with a lot on his shoulders.

"There is no constitutional right to serve in the armed forces," I tell them, reading from the slide. "The presence in the armed forces of persons who demonstrate a propensity or intent to engage in homosexual acts would create an unacceptable risk to the high standards of morale, good order and discipline, and unit cohesion that are the essence of military capability."

I don't mind saying it. It's not masochism; it's relief of pressure, the chance to talk about it, the chance to speak, however bent.

* * *

In December 2010, I am still keeping my hair short on the sides, although now I grow it into a wide, Mohawk-type mess on the top. I'm wearing dress shirts and ties for the first time in my life. But because this is a trendy, modern office (trendy for D.C., at least), I'm not in a suit. Jeans and a button-up aren't out of place here. On Fridays, when it gets casual, I wear a t-shirt, which shows the collection of tattoos I amassed while serving.

Short sleeves in the office bring about another first – being considered butch.

"So you got all your tattoos when you were in the Army?" a member of the field team – the attractive guys and gals who go out to get petitions signed – asks me, as he leans onto my desk and lifts the sleeve of my shirt. "I love guys with tattoos," he says as he smiles before strutting away.

Here in this culture, where everyone is assumed gay first, my tattoos, my novice sense of style and my history in the military present me as almost a tough guy. A little bit butch. Probably a Top.

* * *

In December 2009, I am a superhero.

When soldiers tell people, at least people who live on and around military bases, that they train dogs for the Army, there are only a few responses that they get.

That is so cool. Wow. How did you get into that? So you get to play with dogs every day?

When we're hanging out in our office with our dogs kenneled nearby barking to each other, canine handlers pretend to complain, pretend we've tired of this routine. We haven't. We love the vest with K-9 printed on the back that we wear over our fatigues. We love parking anywhere we please and keeping the oversize SUVs running because we have to keep our eyes on the dogs. We love wrapping our leashes around our shoulders, or letting them hang off of our belts, so that everyone can see them. We like silently encouraging people to ask.

It's the attention. It's the fact that we're being zipped around the world to search for bombs, the fact that we're rubbing elbows with Secret Service in NYC. This feels like rock star status. It's among the reasons that so few handlers are in a rush to leave the military.

"What is it that you think you are you going to do when you get out?" The First Sergeant asked most soldiers to scare them from leaving.

* * *

In December 2010, I am a lackey.

My boss is significantly more butch than I am. No, not butch
– he wears polo shirts tight enough cling to his chest and arms
– but aggressive. From my cubicle outside of his office, I watch
as my coworkers leave conversations with him muttering under
their breath, almost crying sometimes. He doesn't budge. He gets
his way.

"Listen, my friend." One can tell he has distaste for someone
when he calls them "friend."

"That just isn't going to happen."

My job, the job I left the Army for, the job for which I went
to school at night while serving in K-9 units across the globe, is
to keep him happy. Expense reports. Travel arrangements. Find
him a place that ships suits. Call him a taxi.

"Anthony," he calls from his desk, not bothering to stand.
"How about a cupcake run?" Cupcakes for the whole office. He
buys, and I walk down to boutique bakery to pick up our treats.

And here's the thing, as much as this sounds like whining, I
wear a genuine smile as I stand in the brightly lit bakery in Dupont Circle, the historically gay district of the city. I wear tight
slacks and a shirt pinned closed with a skinny tie and balance
several bright pink boxes of 3-dollar-a-piece cupcakes to hand
out to an office full of happy, queer professionals.

* * *

In December 2009, I say K-9. I say SSD. SSG. LP/OP. QRF.
We say FOB, even fobbit. K-pot. CAB. 550 cord. 9 mil. Downrange. FRAGO. XO. BOLO. IED. CBRN or NBC. RPG. Sh-
am-shield. Stripes. NCOIC. MWR. MRE. DFAC. FTX. PX.
M249 Getsome, Getsome.

* * *

In December 2010, I say sexual orientation. I say LGBT.
Try LGBTIQQAA2-S. I say HRC. NCTE. NCLR. HIV/AIDS.
Whitman-Walker. Kinsey. Butler. Sexual orientation. Gen-
der identity. Gender expression. Gender nonconforming. Sec-

ond-parent adoption. Medical power-of-attorney. Civil Union.
SSM. MSM. GLADD and single-D GLAD, NCOD, ENDA,
DADT, DOMA. Repeal, Repeal.

* * *

In December 2009, Staff Sergeant Barrel, the married,
straight soldier who presents the equal opportunity lectures with
me, stands with me in uniform in the hallway of my unit head-
quarters before I walk out the door for the last time. Without any
hush in his voice, he asks me the most personal question he is
permitted to ask me.

"Do you think that they'll repeal it within your lifetime?"

"My lifetime? Of course, two or three more year of this, tops."

"I'm not so sure, there are plenty of old crusty types who are
going to bitch about it."

I nod. "Yeah, but it's not them who gets to decide. This is
going down. We've got a Democrat in the big house and a cam-
paign promise."

He lets a smirk creep out, not a mischievous one, not exactly.
It is something closer to the smile of someone getting away with
something, a whispered ask. "I was half-hoping it would be re-
pealed before you went."

I blush. Despite his benign intent, despite my reemerging
pride, I feel as though I am being accused of something. This
should be the moment in which I come out, at least to a soldier I
trust, when the stakes are low.

I don't.

* * *

In December 2010, I am sitting in meeting space on the first
floor of building where I work in D.C. The space is all glass and
milky white surfaces, floor-to-ceiling windows, plenty of light.
Today there are rows of chairs and a projection screen set up for
those of us who aren't down the street watching firsthand the
President sign this bill into law.

I've been misty-eyed all day. I could barely keep it together on the subway train in, so I know that I might lose it when the livestream starts. I sit in the back with a cup of coffee, my legs crossed as I lean forward at the edge of my seat. I've got a lot on my to-do list today: expense reports, blogs posts. A celebratory cupcake run, no doubt. Still, today they will cut me some slack.

As the stream begins, we watch as the camera scans the crowd. The gay congressman is there. There's the Arabic linguist who the Army asked to leave, and the pilot kicked out just before retirement. There's Eric, who lost his leg during the first push into Iraq.

"Hey Anthony," a blond coworker with a sweet face and kind, blue eyes sits down beside me in a T-shirt that reads REPEAL THE BAN. "Didn't you used to be in the military?"

"Yeah," I tell him. "Used to."

I smile with some resignation, keeping my eyes on the screen as they well up. I smile with a small amount of embarrassment, with a small amount of pride. As the morning sun slips in through the window behind my seat, I smile, out of uniform.

"Thank you. Thank you," the President begins. "Today is a good day."

TO AMERICA
by Lizbeth Prifogle

SEPTEMBER 2008

"How was it?" people ask, smiling. They talk to me as if they are connected to the war in Iraq. Connected to the service that they were too lazy, too undisciplined, too political, too whatever to join themselves.

"Hot and sandy," I answer, refusing to feed their idea of glorified war, already reinforced daily by MSNBC, CNN, Fox News, and more.

"Oh," they reply, the smile fading from their face when I give them a cold stare to make them wonder if I killed any hajjis, ragheads, camel jockeys, sand niggers, or any of the other offensive terms we are taught to call the people we are at war with in order to dehumanize them until they become our enemy. "Are you going to have to go back?" they ask with dramatic sympathy. It's as if I am awaiting orders for either parole or execution. They never consider that we don't mind going. That this is our job, our choice, what we do to pay our bills, feed our kids, pay off expensive college loans. Civilians don't understand that we are Marines, we don't need pity when we deploy – it's what we are trained to do, what we volunteer to do.

"I don't know. It depends on what unit I'm with after I PCS

or if I can get attached to a team on an IA billet." I throw out as many terms and acronyms as I can to boggle their civilian brains.

Again, a blank stare. I don't explain that PCS means Permanent Change of Duty Station or that IA billet means Individual Augment. Both mean you're assigned to a different unit, mission, people, maybe even a different war.

"Do you want to go back?" they ask, ignoring my acronyms.

"I wouldn't mind going to Afghanistan," I answer out of habit. I have learned that the crazier I make myself appear, the fewer inappropriate personal questions they ask.

They change the subject when they realize they can't empathize with my response. Instead, they focus on simple things, like the weather.

"How hot was it?" Their relentless curiosity about a world they will never experience should be flattering, but instead it makes me sick to my stomach like I'm caught in a sandstorm and inhaling too much dust again.

"The week before I left we had a barbecue and at twenty hundred, I mean 8 PM, it was still 110 degrees outside. It was at least 115 during the day. On our way home we had to stop in Kuwait for four days. There it was closer to like 120."

I don't tell them it snowed in January. It's not my job to fix their misconceptions.

"Wow, that's hot," they say in their most enthusiastic voice. I don't remind them that under flak jackets and Kevlar helmets, carrying a daypack, rifle, and pistol that it's more than hot - it's fucking unbearable.

They ask about the sandstorms, the bombings, the people, but all they know of war are images from television and retold stories from nephews, distant cousins, or someone who knew someone who went over there at some point.

"Yeah. It's hot," I shrug.

I didn't used to be this cynical or this brazen. I don't feel salty or even sad. It's like I no longer live my life and instead watch it through a television screen waiting for the character that looks like me, sounds like me, but isn't really me to react to the various situations invisible producers create from an office off-set.

My friends try to be supportive, but don't get that the only support I need is to be left alone. They volunteer to help move my stuff out of storage – stuff I don't want anymore – but I tell them I can manage on my own and hire movers with the money I saved up over the deployment. As I unpack, I wonder why I bought this stuff in the first place, clothes and trinkets that once had meaning, jewelry and coins that I insured for their value. It all seems like a burden to move into my latest temporary living arrangement. I dream of giving everything I own to the homeless man on the corner of my new neighborhood who stands at the intersection and holds a sign every night that reads:

"Homeless Vet suffering from PMSD:
Post-Marriage-Stress-Disorder"

But his grocery cart is already full; he doesn't have room for my trash too. I roll down my window and give him all my cash and spare change instead. A friend comments that he probably spends it on booze. Good for him, I think as I roll up my car window without smiling and turn the corner, watching the man count out my spare change in the rear-view mirror. He always looks disappointed in my charity of leftovers from the day's expenses. Sometimes he throws the coins at my car and screams expletives. I simply drive on, happy that I'm not the only one having a bad day.

It's only been three weeks since I arrived back in the states. I spent six months in a combat zone and what do I have to show for it? A couple more medals and ribbons to pin on my Dress Blues. Cheap souvenirs from the various "hajji shops" on base that I toss in boxes labeled "shit I don't need." Bags under my eyes from insomnia. A headache from another hangover.

My friends drag me out so they can brag and tell strangers I'm a Marine and I was in Iraq. That I was there and now I'm home. "Safe," they announce to their captive audience. People thank me, shake my hand, and buy a round of drinks.

"No thanks, I'm good," I say, but another beer and shot are ordered anyways.

The strangers ask, "So, how was it?" with a tone in their voice like they are good listeners. Like I can finally tell them the truth instead of some patriotic, bullshit canned answer they've heard so many times before. Like I can confide in them and share the sins I carry alone so as not to burden loved ones. The bar is loud and they are drunk and I consider bearing my soul, if for nothing else than to get them to leave me alone.

"It's over," I say as I raise the shot glass of unknown liquor to cheers. "To America," I announce, feigning hope. I gulp the alcohol I didn't want. It burns my throat, and for a second my numb body tingles.

"To being home!" they add as they slam the small glass on the counter.

After an awkward pause, they finally leave to talk to a prettier, friendlier girl at the other end of the bar.

* * *

Therapy
June 2013

I accidentally started therapy a year ago.

"Let's talk about grieving," my therapist says from across the room.

I smile, a trick I learned as a shy child. Being a thirty year old combat vet in therapy hasn't changed my best line of defense. In fact it's made it more convincing – it's no longer an innocent kid hiding behind a sweet smile, but a woman who is disarmingly quiet with a thousand yard stare, all masked by a practiced response. Unfortunately, this doesn't work on my therapist the way it does to strangers in dim-lit bars.

I thought she was a vocational counselor when I met her at a mandatory Individual Ready Reserve muster two years after I left active duty. The following week when I walked into her office and saw the fake plants and heard the soft sounds of crashing waves from a hidden stereo, I realized she wasn't going to help me with my resume.

As I stare and smile, shadows from the late afternoon sun pass through the soft, iridescent curtains into the sterile room. She's added plants and soft lighting, but it's still a government owned facility. She waits for a response to regain control of the conversation. I wait until she looks down at her notes trying to figure out a different way to ask me the same question.

"I went to a memorial service when a Marine officer was killed in Iraq," I blurt out like a child running through her day's events at the supper table. "I didn't know him, but the whole base was invited so I went." I leave out that I pretended to be an investigative journalist to pass the time during the quiet deployment. I even kept a blog about life in a war zone for a handful of followers who stumbled upon the page, but the most interesting subject I was allowed to write about was my ongoing obsession with running. I don't tell her that I took a massive, digital SLR camera to the memorial service to play this pretend role, and capture this side of war. I hold onto my secret. I didn't feel grief, but such shame that I left as they sang the last hymns and said the last prayers. I had never met him, but saw this as an opportunity to run for my pretend Pulitzer Prize.

That week, I blogged about the marathon I was training for.

She doesn't say anything. A moment passes and she looks down at her notebook again.

"About a year ago, a captain that I used to hang out with died in Afghanistan. I didn't really know him either, but he was the housemate of an ex-boyfriend. I didn't go to any memorials or anything, but I remember reading about it online. It still seems strange that I knew him and now he's just gone." My voice trails off as I watch her entire body relax. This is the most I've ever revealed during a session. "That's it really. My dad's mom passed recently, but I never met her. All my other grandparents and family I do know are all still living. People always tell me I'm lucky, but it's not luck. They're all going to die someday. Waiting isn't lucky." I catch myself rambling and shift my posture to cross my legs and arms.

At my first appointment, I actually had a copy of my resume in hand. For the first six months, she helped me navigate the VA disability claim process – not a small feat. Then it was just habit to make my next appointment at the end of the hour. She tells me she's treating me for "transition disorder," even though I returned from Iraq more than three years ago.

"Are there any other relationships that ended and you had to grieve? Boyfriends or friends?"

I think of my past relationships. They never lasted long and usually ended in an unspoken mutual agreement. Friendships and boyfriends all come in and out of my life quick and quiet. I recognized that our roles in one another's lives had been fulfilled.

I sit and study the mundane, government furnished carpet, forgetting to answer her question. The office buildings on base were covered in the exact shade of cobalt blue carpet.

"No?" She asks.

The fake birds chirp from her cd player and a little patch of sun hits my bare thighs and draws my attention. I notice goose bumps popping up on my soft skin like tiny sand dunes emerging on a barren landscape. I scratch at them.

When I finally received my disability letter from the VA, we both cheered in her little office. I remember thinking afterwards what a funny thing to cheer about. My final diagnosis was: Post Traumatic Stress Disorder (also claimed as depression and anxiety). Getting the government's recognition was a bittersweet victory, especially considering the hours spent submitting medical documentation and sitting with various doctors reliving the trauma.

"Well, I want to specifically talk about a loss of oneself. Do you think you are the same person you were before you joined the marines?"

"No. Of course not," I unintentionally roll my eyes.

She wants to save me. I can see that she feels like she can save every veteran if given a cape, the ability to fly, and all the

time in the world. I respect her for her sincere passion and dedication, but I don't want to be saved – not like this.

"Ok, good. Do you like the person you've become?"

I fight the urge to become hostile. "What the fuck kind of
question is that?" I want to snap like an angry teenager, but she
has never been anything but kind to me. Instead, I simply shrug
my shoulders and say, "I am who I am. It simply is what it is now."

I hate the cliché phrase that has become an answer for everything, from the meaning of life to receiving a moldy pastry at a
café. I hate that while it has become an everyday phrase, it's true
– it is what it is, I am who I am now.

I don't like who I have become. I don't like the chemicals I
was exposed to, the vaccines they injected in my bloodstream, my
acceptance of killing another human being in the name of war.
War. For an act so big, the word just seems too small. No, I don't
like Captain Prifogle who sits in therapy out of habit. I like Libby,
but she's a POW or MIA. The war has long since ended, but I'm
still waiting for the body to wash up on shore so I can give her a
proper burial.

She pauses and lets me reflect for a moment. I let the silence
wash over me like a crashing wave on jagged rocks. The cold dis-
comfort of who I've become envelopes my skin, seeping into my
bones. I catch a glimmer of the emotional being I once was and
a chill runs down my spine. My whole body trembles like I'm
having a petit mal seizure as the wave washes Libby back to sea.
My stomach burns as sand enters the cracks and crevices of the
stonewall Captain Prifogle pretends to be.

What she doesn't get is that I need to be the hero of my story,
not a damsel in distress needing rescue by a motherly shrink.

"You need to mourn the person you were," my therapist in-
terjects, ending our staring contest. "You can never be that person
again and you need to mourn that loss in order to accept who
you have become." She starts reading the names and definitions
of the universal stages of grief. Her voice is flat, like I just need to
put a check in each box and move on to the next: denial, anger,

bargaining, depression, and acceptance. She makes it sound like a simple equation: giving up 24 years of being Libby + stages of grief = moving on.

I wonder if this will last forever. Will she just keep making appointments in a sad attempt to rescue me? Will I just keep showing up because of my OCD we haven't discussed yet?

"You're so much stronger now," she says with a go team go flare.

Everyone says this. When I jolt up from nightmares and reach for my pistol, or have a sudden unexplainable panic attack in a crowd. "You're so strong now," they tell me like it's a goddamn consolation prize. "You're so strong," they say, but what they really mean is, "you're a Marine, I thought you were supposed to be tough and fearless." They always use that word, strong.

Yes, I'm stronger now. The Marine Corps made me tough. Strong enough to stifle the emotions that used to make me human. Tough enough to beat out the individuality that made me Libby. Yes, I'm fucking strong. I'm "step right up and see the strongest women in the world" strong. But nobody tells you what the cost of this strength is. Nobody tells you that you have to be stronger than who you were so you can kill her. I was tricked. Now I have to mourn the person I was and I didn't even give her a fighting chance. She had strengths too, they were just different.

I'm waiting on her to give up on me. I've withdrawn so much that everyone else has given up and moved on, why can't she?

I think about Libby. The girl who dyed her hair purple because she thought it was pretty and brought out her green eyes. The girl who didn't walk through the grocery store, but tap danced through the aisles for no reason other than she really liked to tap dance. The girl with so much energy that her dad nicknamed her Tigger. Libby, the girl who was brave enough to move to Scotland and then later to New York City; both times she was flat broke, but fearless and faithful. She knew the universe would provide and she was grateful that it always did. Happy, but physically weak and emotional.

I think about Captain Prifogle. The woman who joined the

Marines because her dad told her she wouldn't make it. The woman who learned military tactics and how to give a five paragraph order like she was ordering a meal. The woman who led Marines in a combat zone; who shouted "kill" over and over and over again until killing another human being wasn't questioned by her instinct for survival of the species. The Marine who runs marathons, lifts weights, has a sculpted body, knows how to kill someone with just her hands and given the right circumstances would execute without a second thought. She appears strong and callous, but is broken and sad. Some days the weight of her decisions and the things she saw are too heavy to carry and she can't get out of bed. On those days she thinks of the rock biter from the NeverEnding Story. She remembers the scene after The Nothing swept away all of his friends and left him helpless and alone. He looks at his hands and says, "They look like big, good, strong hands, don't they? I always thought that's what they were." The Nothing has taken Libby and no matter how resilient Captain Prifogle appears to be, she's left with nothing but big, lumpy, rock hands.

But I am strong now.

"We're not the people we used to be and we need to accept who we are," my therapist says as a soft acoustic guitar plays over a flowing river in the background. She likes to remind me that she is also a veteran. I like to remind myself that she was in civil affairs and instead of trained to kill, she was trained to help.

I bite the side of my tongue because the pain occupies my mind and stops me from crying. I don't want to mourn the person I was before the Marine Corps. I knew and liked her. I don't know this person that wakes up every morning at 0430 and inventories the lines on her face. Who is this person who goes to work in drab colored clothes and does what she's told in order to collect a paycheck? I don't like this woman who can't remember the last time she sat with her sisters and laughed until she snorted, or tap danced through the grocery store.

"Ok, I think that we've gone over enough today, when do you want to make your next appointment?" My therapist closes her PTSD guidebook and opens her monthly calendar. I take a long, deep breath, and let out a sigh of relief. I schedule my next appointment to visit Libby in the cold, dark prison holding her on an indefinite sentence.

She walks me to the front office. I say goodbye to the veteran, student-workers at the front desk who look younger and younger each month. They all smile too.

I drive home breaking the speed limit and swerving in and out of lanes. What I don't say in therapy is that sometimes I wish I had died in combat. I wake up. I go to work. I do what I'm supposed to do, and in the quiet of the afternoon I daydream of a world without me. Who would fill my position at work? Would my boyfriend be dating someone else? How would my life be memorialized on Veteran's Day in my small, Indiana hometown? I dream of a world where I died as a hero. A world where my life had purpose. I dream about how others would grieve me - not the woman I've become, but the girl they knew. The girl who didn't train her mind to kill in the name of war. The girl who laughed, explored, and wrote obsessively in her journals. If I die now, I'll be a blurb in the San Diego Union Tribune and the lives of those around me.

Of course, I'm not waiting for my therapist to give up on me. I'm waiting for Captain Prifogle to give up on Libby. Why won't she accept that Libby is never leaving the internment camp holding her?

I make it home safe in spite of myself. I open a journal I haven't touched in months. I write the date and time and scribble out my answer:

I can't grieve the person I was because she's still out there. Everyone else has moved on so it's up to me to find her...

The following month, I forget to go to my appointment. My therapist never calls to reschedule.

OBLIVION
by Adam Stone

T hrough my scope I see him standing there, on the brink of oblivion. I imagine he is contemplating his existence, whether to take that step. He sways with the mild wind allowing its breeze to caress him like a mother rocks her child. He looks over his shoulder as if to see if someone was there to give him encouragement; there is no one!

I imagine he is alone in this world, and this is his only way. As he turns, the look in his eyes has changed, no longer is it fear; but that of determination. He takes the step. I lean closer as if to be able to stop him, I scream in my head for him to go back. My hand instinctively reaches out as though I could push him backwards from over five hundred yards away. I close my eyes, cringing at the anticipation of the commotion that is about to occur. Deafening silence! I strengthen in my resolve and look back through the scope, watching him, walk towards me.

I have trained for twenty years to survive in a combat situation. How to fight, to read others, to determine if they are a threat. I've trained for decades to strengthen my mind and body. I've mastered the art of hand-to-hand combat, I can accurately shoot my rifle and side arm with near pinpoint accuracy. I have learned to numb my emotions by the loss my closest friend, and seeing what my own rifle can do to the enemy. I can shoot a man in the center of his chest from five hundred yards away, and put a knife thru his throat so close I can count of cavities in his mouth. I've gone through psychological profiles before and after every combat tour to ensure I can still be considered sane.

As he walked toward me, all my years of training, my decades of experience, vanished like smoke in a breeze. I was lost in a sea of emotion. There he was, a child no older than my 13 year old son, walking towards me, but not to me. He was walking to a discarded vehicle left in the middle of an ancient mine field. A leftover from a past war, a constant reminder of the horrors this country has seen.

He walks with purpose. Knowing that if he makes it to that shattered hulk eroding in the sand he might be able to find something he can sell to the Taliban. He knows that the price is high. The bigger the item, the more destructive it can be, the better off he will be. An old artillery shell can feed him for a month, but anything salvaged can feed him for the day, possibly a week.

He knows that the Marines guarding the small outpost, just five hundred yards away, are authorized to shoot and kill anyone they deem a threat. His livelihood depends on what he finds, just as the weapon he wears across his back is his way to survive. He's been raised here, and he knows that there is safety in the field that has seen so much death. Many have tried before him; the field is strewn with the signs of those that have failed, shreds of cloth here, a crater there, even a shoe or two are scattered about. He knows that where death once was, he is safe. A land mine can only explode once.

He arrives at a crater and jumps inside, resting for a moment, kneeling down as if to pray to his god to give him the strength to continue his journey. As he hunkers down into the depression, I see my own children playing at the beach, building sand castles and burying each other, laughing as they run and jump into holes not much different from the one the child I see is resting in now; only three hundred yards from my position.

From this distance, I can easily hit the target. The wind is slightly blowing from right to left; the sun is behind me erasing all shadows and highlighting my target. In actuality it would be an easy shot, and be justified under the rules of engagement. As I sight in on the boy, I make the appropriate adjustments to my rifle. I firmly grasp the pistol grip, pulling it slightly toward me, ensuring the stalk of the weapon is comfortably in the pocket of my shoulder. I rest the barrel of my weapon in the palm of my forward hand allowing it to just lay there until the moment is necessary. My trigger finger hovers next to the trigger, waiting for the moment. My shooting position is perfect. No one, no one, would question why I pulled the trigger.

I would more than likely get a few "good jobs" and "wows" from the younger, less seasoned Marines, who talk openly about seeing action, and wanting to shoot something other than a paper target. Young Marines, who have been raised in front of a television screen, playing "Modern Warfare" in simulated battles around the world.

Who also tend to treat life as just another simulation. But there is no reset button, no pause, and no cheat codes. I hold my position, watching the target with my finger next to the trigger.

He lifts himself out of his hole and stands at the threshold. His prize, a mere fifty yards away. But it might as well be one hundred, one thousand, or even ten thousand. For the distance isn't the problem, it's what's between and underneath. He takes a step and begins to walk again. As he moves, his eyes are ever vigilant, shifting, searching for a tell in the sand of possible danger. Nothing can be seen. Footstep after footstep his body tenses as it might be his last.

I can see him clearer now. The sweat of his brow, the dirt on his face, and even the beginnings of manhood as a slight wispy mustache is starting to darken above his lip. I can also see he is no stranger to war: A ragged scar runs from where his left ear should be to the corner of his mouth. He is missing two fingers from his left hand, and I postulate that the entire left side of his body is battle damaged in some way. Possibly the effects of a land mine he was fortunate to walk away from, more than likely, as I have seen too many times, when he was an infant, his mother shielded him from danger, protecting him, with her own body, leaving scars as a reminder of her love. I watch closely, he is just 25 yards away.

His pace is slow and methodical, choosing each step carefully. I again reminisce about my children when I send them to bed for the evening. The slow intentional walk down the hall, hoping a reprieve might come, allowing them to watch just one more show. No reprieve ever comes for them, nor will there be for the boy who rests squarely in my sights.

He is only yards away, the fruit of his labors within his grasp. My body stiffens, ready to shoot. He climbs into the mangled mass of the vehicle whose ancient armor shields him from my sight.

The world envelopes me; behind me I can hear the distant sound of music playing on a radio. Marines on a break from what lies outside our walls are playing cards to occupy their minds. The smell of baked chicken being prepared for the evening meal lofts up to me, and for a moment I can relax and take in the world.

(Tick….Tick….Tick) The hours of the second hand slowly pass.

When I see the boy exiting the vehicle, I am funneled back into the reality that lay in my sights. In his hands is a wooden box, filled with miscellaneous wires and pieces of scrap metal. Resting on top is his personal fortune. A cylindrical shaped object that resembles an old Soviet mortar shell. The boy doesn't waste any time, he begins crossing the field as fast as possible attempting to retrace his steps that had brought him to his treasure trove.

(Thud, Thud, Thud) The emptying and filling of my heart is now keeping time.

I tighten in my position, ensuring I can get a clean shot. The boy has now become the enemy. Never mind the rifle he wears across his back—every six year old in this country has one—the mortar shell, if sold to the Taliban, can be used against the Marines and soldiers in the field. He moves quickly; I adjust for his speed, my finger slips into the trigger well. I can feel the warmth of the indifferent steel as I apply slight pressure; my weapon is ready. He reaches the crater where I imagined him praying, and he abruptly stops. He's frozen, not a muscle is moving. Can he feel the barrel of my rifle bearing down on him? He's motionless. Beads of sweat roll down the back of his neck. He's breathing heavily, he stands for what seems like eternity.

(Click) I apply more pressure to the trigger. He slowly lowers the box of goods, down from his chest, and looks up to the sky.

(Click) I place my thumb on the safety, ready to unleash the dogs of war.

BOOM.

The outpost siren is wailing; every Marine from around the compound stops what they are doing and rushes to the perimeter with a rifle in hand to defend our position. It takes the cloud of sand and debris from the explosion ten minutes to finally settle. After a few minutes, the all clear sounds and everyone goes back to what they were doing before. The music starts to play, the games continue, and I helplessly look out across the field of oblivion.

A torrent of emotion swells, I'm confused; was that me? No, my weapon is still on safe. Where's the boy? He's gone. I…am thankful; it wasn't me, I didn't have to, I would have, I could have, this time—THIS TIME!—it wasn't my choice. My soul, though empty, is still intact. I am angry and demoralized. I understand why the boy made the trek, all this child wanted was to live, to survive. I think of all the children that have crossed my path. The ones on the side of the road begging for change, the ones in the refugee camps, waiting in never-ending lines, even the ones that have stolen from me. They all had one thing in common: the will to survive. That boy was doing what he had to do, to survive. He was looking for a way to survive for more than just today, but so he wouldn't have to walk through a minefield tomorrow.

As I walk off the plane two months later, I see my children standing there on the edge of runway. I couldn't help but think of the boy and his trek, and all that had happened.

I have killed, I have hurt others, justified or not, but I have also loved and cared for my enemy as I have loved and cared for my own children. Now they are all here, together, running to me.

FAREWELL DEAR GHOST
by Eric Strand

S omeone once tried to measure the mass of the soul by
weighing people when they died.

When you died, I barely noticed that you had
changed. It was your strange familiarity that made me
pause and rustle your hair in the brief moment before I zipped
the bag over your face.

Returning to the bloodied soil you had just left, the groans
of the wounded drowned out the weight your leaving soul had
placed on mine.

The single tear that I choked back as I watched the helicopter
blades make beautiful paintings in the red smoke was no indica-
tion of a future of what it truly means to be haunted by a ghost.

We were close, but others were closer. No matter what other
relationships you had before, nothing will change the fact that
the universe tilted slightly on the day that you traded your life
for mine.

You were with me, watching our daughters play together later
that summer, me deciding that I've had enough, that I should
finally get an education. The nights where you would take advantage of those vulnerable moments before sleep and transmit
to me the feeling of dying just outside of reach, yet a world away

from your brothers. Those nights when you showed me the lonely feeling of gasping for last breaths under dark, dusty skies.

I know that we all pay homage to your memory one way in public and quite another in the quiet moments when we lose control of our thoughts. But whatever growing weight your soul presses on us all, there is too much tragedy in this world for one person to sustain.

So, I am sorry, my dear friend, I cannot bear the burden of your haunting any more.

There is no fixed amount of tragedy in this world; the measure I bear lifts no weight from others. I must let our time together as spectre and survivor pass to make good with grace the gift of this life you have given me.

It doesn't mean we were not friends or brothers, you and I. I only ask that you let a portion of your increasingly heavy soul drift into the bending light as I face forward into the uncertain number of sunrises that you granted me. For guilt is the enemy of gratitude, sleepless nights are the enemy of well-lived days, and feeling unworthy closes all doors to love.

Finally, rest well, and thank you.

I WRITE TO YOU FROM KANDAHAR AGAIN

By Mariah Smith

I write to you from Kandahar again.

Last time we saw this place together was February of 2011. Do you remember how crowded the Boardwalk was? We were traveling to the Purple Heart ceremony down in Tarin Kowt. It was winter and we were fighting the weather. We'd made it into Kandahar by C-130, then six flights in a row were scratched. Six trips down to the PAX terminal. Hopes dashed six times. Six times three hours wasted in manifesting for helicopters that never showed.

Eventually we sat in the Chili's—who'd have thought there would be a Chili's here? Or a Boardwalk?—playing Scrabble, desperate to kill time. I started to cry. Scared and feeling hopeless that we were going to miss seeing the survivors. We'd miss seeing their faces and shaking their hands, comforted in the tangible proof that they were intact, in body certainly, if not in spirit. You paused in your act of setting down a letter A, looking at me across the table. Concern written across your face.

Later we walked the boardwalk and took pictures of the gray tabby cat who had made himself a little cave in the exact middle of a pallet of water bottles, sleeping curled with his paw over his nose for warmth.

One night and then a second, spent shivering miserably in the temporary billets. I'd committed the unpardonable sin of traveling in country without my poncho liner, despite knowing better. Why is the AC on in winter? I pictured the many past nights I'd spent sweating on a cot draped in mosquito net. I huddled, too cold to truly fall asleep even with my watch cap. At some point in the night I felt someone lean over me and cover me with an old wool army blanket. A brief glimpse in the dark of a tan T-shirt and braids pulled back into a bun. I woke long enough to hold my teeth together from chattering and murmured a "Thank you." In the morning, all other transient soldiers were gone so I didn't even have a chance to thank her again. I folded the Army blanket at the foot of the bare plastic mattress and left it for the next stranded traveler.

Eventually, after 48 hours, a helicopter came. I have always loved Chinooks best of all, those big ugly workhorses with their deep, reassuring chop. I wanted to be a pilot like you but it wasn't in the cards. As soon as we were on the bird they hustled us right back off, a soldier running back on with a clipboard, papers flapping. There was some mistake. Maybe. They weren't sure. They ushered everyone off. I stood my ground, pointing to you, grabbing the crew chief's harness to shout into his headset. Everything deafened by the rotor wash. Your Kevlar-topped face peering in, worried, from the yawning ramp of the bird.

"That's my Dad," I hollered into the crew chief's headset. "We're trying to get to my husband's outpost for his Purple Heart ceremony."

The crew chief stared at me for a minute, taking this in, his face almost completely hidden by his helmet. I didn't let go of his harness until I saw understanding in his eyes and he waved you back on. We buckled in. We made it in time. Just barely.

That was three winters ago and that was my fifth tour. Kandahar is a ghost town now. The Forever War is waning, for the time being. I can't believe I'm here again. Scratch that, yes I can. I feel like I never left. Like the three years between tours five and six were the dream and this is the only reality. Like my short marriage was just a dream too. Like too many other veterans, it was lost to the never ending pace of the back-to-back deployments and the uncertainty and absence of stability. And the fact that even when I was home part of me was still always here. War was over for him and he was ready for it to be over for me too, but many of us can't leave it behind and when we get a chance to come back and live it again, we go.

I'm here with a different unit, a different set of people. I find myself becoming confused at which tours I've gone through with which friends. I turn to SFC Carter smiling to reminisce about how this drive reminds me of the time we drove from Ghazni to Camp Warehouse in Kabul and stopped for a lunch of goat and watermelon with the Afghan National Police at the camp named Four Corners. But that wasn't him. That was a different year, a different sector, the same war, a different me.

The news rattles incessantly from one of four flat screens mounted in the TOC. How people return to their narrow metal rooms and continue to watch TV well into the night is beyond me. The voices are deafening. The words never stop. More responsibility and thus more clamor every day. I am constantly surrounded by sound and smothered with interaction until after 16-18 hours of it each day I retreat behind a locked door for 6 hours to write or better yet, read, in as much silence as I can muster.

I'm exhausted but strangely happy, even after I discovered Tim Robbins donuts was gone from the Boardwalk. There aren't as many Canadians here anymore as there were last time and I miss them. Last time I saw Kandahar it was a zoo of different uniforms, concrete barriers and strange vehicles parked in every available spot. Jostling constantly for room in the showers, in the line at the chow hall, in the gym.

Now it is empty and makes sense. I can see the neat grid squares of space as it was originally laid out. Entire yards sit empty, the green sniper netting torn and dusty, peeling away to blow across the scrubby no-man's land. We now have a wealth of space.

In the mornings I walk outside of our small compound within a compound and stand under the bay trees with my coffee. It took me weeks to figure out what these trees were, the smell oddly familiar from my childhood. I finally placed it one day when I fished out a familiar leaf from the stew at the mess hall.

There won't be a normal for me. This isn't an interlude from my regular life. This is my life. Normal has passed me by. Who will I be when I am no longer at war? I'm 36. This all started when I was 22, a platoon leader. Two planes flew into two towers and two more planes went down and not too much later I was standing in a surprise formation watching a general from the 101st give us our go-to-war speech. My friends all are married with kids now. I love them just the same as I always have, but our common ground is fading.

I know you would have come with me this time if you could. I love you and I wish you were here to see this. Everything is closing down here. We will be one of the last units out. And then we will wait until we get told to go somewhere else. From what I see on the TVs, I doubt we will have to wait long. I am glad. I feel useful. But someday there will be a pause in this long war and I will have to search out a new way to find meaning in my days. But what will ever come close to this? I look at the faces around me. They grow younger with every tour. This is all new for them. They make me smile. I don't need to be anywhere else. For now, I am home.

BECOMING A VETERAN
by Samuel Chamberlain

I don't remember being born and the first half-decade of my life is just a blur, which is how I feel about my initial days home from the war. I know there was a welcome home ceremony. I know I stood in formation, at the position of attention, wearing my maroon beret. I know there came a point where a general officer congratulated us for a job well done and then asked the anxious families to greet their soldier. I'm six foot three and stood half a head above many of the paratroopers in formation—my wife saw me from afar and rushed through the crowd to embrace me, her husband, her veteran.

It was Thanksgiving weekend and upon leaving the reception we were given a four-day pass. I don't remember eating turkey or ham or mashed potatoes with gravy or cranberry sauce or pies. Those first days home I don't think I left my condo. I'm sure I enjoyed my queen size bed. I'm sure I made love to my wife. I'm sure I drank.

There were two photographs taken that first long weekend of my homecoming. One is of my wife and I, smiling, embracing at the Fort Richardson gymnasium after the redeployment ceremony. The second photograph is my dog and I—a white Alaskan husky named Jasper—rolling on the floor together. My recollection of those first days home probably come from these photographs; my memory has faded to impressions, uncomplicated emotions, oversimplified adjectives. I was home from war, but what hadn't struck me yet was that I was a veteran.

For Christmas that year my parents gave me a lifetime membership to the VFW. An organization my grandfather had been an active member of throughout his life. For me it was just a cheap bar. I didn't feel part of the same legacy. I'd done fifteen months. I'd spent every day outside the wire on hundreds of missions in the Sunni-Shia triangle of death. I had a combat patch for being over there and a combat badge for being in the shit, but none of that made me feel like a veteran yet.

I spent two more years in uniform before deciding I wasn't a lifer. I chose to stay in Alaska--my duty station--over the Army. I chose peace with my wife over dedication to duty. When they know you're on your way out, the lifers start to treat the short timers with a different attitude. They start to make you question your decision by insinuating whatever you plan to do next will never be as good as the Army.

I evaluated my skills--jumping out of airplanes (at night and in the snow); proficiency on a variety of weapons systems including the M4, M9, M249, and M2; as a Sapper I knew how to blow up bridges, blow up buildings, blow up trees, blow up obstacles, and how to find, avoid, and disarm dangerous IEDs by blowing them up; as a leader I cared for my men, coordinated indirect fires, coordinated rotary wing and fixed wing close air support, and interacted with an Arabic interpreter—and transitioned into the most likely of follow-up careers; I became a middle school English teacher.

I think I wanted to become a teacher for the same reason I wanted to be a soldier: adventure. Though I came to believe in ideas like selflessness, honor, courage, and respect, initially I was motivated by adventure. And though I would come to know teaching as a similarly selfless profession that required patience, assertiveness, and a calm demeanor—like I had honed in combat—it was really the challenge I sought. I took a position with the Yukon Flats School District in the rural community of Arctic Village, Alaska.

Arctic Village is located over a hundred miles north of the Arctic Circle. Only accessible by plane, it's a two-hour flight in an eleven seat Cessna Grand Caravan, 240 miles away from Fairbanks, the closest place resembling an urban cityscape. Arctic Village is home to approximately 130 people, all native Alaskans, Gwich'in, the people of the caribou. The community is situated in a valley on the East Fork of the Chandalar River, surrounded on one side by Alaska's northernmost mountain range, the Brooks, and on the other by low rolling hills of tundra sloping downwards for a hundred miles to the Yukon River. The snow came in September, and by the time school got out in May, the river was still locked in ice. Summer days were truly endless and for thirty days each winter we never saw the sun. Twenty students, fifth through twelfth grade, filled my classroom. I was responsible with teaching them English, mathematics, and electives like PE and art.

At first, around the community, I was greeted as, "the new teacher," usually followed by a stare or impartial welcome. A lot of bush teachers don't last long. Many quit in the first few months, a few never return from Christmas exodus, and there were stories of some taking the "midnight express" and leaving their classrooms suddenly vacant the next school day. Because the attrition rate is so high, jobs are readily available in bush Alaska. It was as far from the Army as I could possibly get.

The second week I lived in Arctic Village an elder died through a sudden and tragic accident. I never knew the man, but in the months afterwards I was told, "You would have liked Albert Joe." And that, "Albert Joe would have liked you." They described how young at heart he was and how he taught new teachers the ways of the land. He took them hunting. He took them trapping. He took them fishing. He was a veteran.

Albert Joe's widow requested military rites since he'd served in the Navy. But the Navy wasn't going to send a squad of sailors to this remote region, even if it was the last request for the family of a comrade. Only one plane flies to Arctic Village per day. If the weather is poor, meaning, if clouds blow in and limit visibility, planes won't land. August in Arctic Village is like late fall in the Shenandoah mountains where I grew up. The tundra turns a fiery red. The alders and willows growing along the riverbank golden, much like the Appalachian's maples and oaks. The nights are cool and the smell of wood smoke lingers through the day.

Somehow word spread that I was a veteran, a fact not obvious by my outward appearance--I was beginning to look more like an aspiring hippy than a soldier--when several men from the village asked me to participate in the funeral honors. I was taken aback. With war a constant part of my five-year career, I'd been to many funerals, so many I'd lost count. It was part of my duty, homage. We wore the same uniform. Whether we were in the same unit or not. We were at war in Iraq and Afghanistan. Men died. I could've too. But during my five years as an officer I'd never participated in a 21-gun salute, though several times I'd had the duty of presenting a neatly folded flag to the next of kin, bending at the waist in full dress uniform, old glory grasped between white-gloved hands, reciting, "On behalf of a grateful nation..." to the widow.

The day of the Albert Joe's service, we spent the morning rehearsing with our 30-30-lever actions. They were hunting rifles. The seven of us looked more like members of a rustic militia than a funeral detail. "Wear something military looking," one member of the funeral party had suggested.

I dug through the few belongings I'd brought to the village and found a black baseball cap, Sapper tab stenciled across the front, something I'd purchased after graduating from one of the Army's hardest schools. Seeing it again not only reminded me of who I used to be, but also that I could do anything, notions I would need to muster teaching teenagers. Along with my green, brown, and black woodland camouflage gore tex jacket, it would be my funeral detail uniform.

The graveyard sat high on a cut bank above the river, the village's oldest spruce-log cabins less than a quarter mile away. I lined up with the six others, all dark-skinned natives, and I thought about what we had in common. They'd all decided to become a part of something greater than themselves. In my mind there's a photograph of us, proud men wearing piecemeal camouflage and an assortment of veteran's ball caps. One man, the village's first chief, wore a black leather jacket with a giant eagle embroidered on the back. The eagle's beak agape, screaming a constant war cry. I didn't know where these men served or what they did, nor did it matter.

We stood at attention. I gave the command, "Port, ARMS," and the group followed with the three-count movement, finishing with rifles grasped in front of chests. I gave the command, "Present, ARMS" and the rifles were lowered and rotated, arms partially outstretched, elbows locked, barrels parallel to our bodies, muzzles at eye level. I ordered us back to "Port, ARMS," and the men knew it was almost time to fire our volley. We turned a half step to the left, our muzzles pointed skyward at a forty-five degree angle, northward and away into the Arctic National Wildlife Refuge. There are no blank 30-30 rounds in Arctic Village; our rifles were loaded with real bullets. I gave the command, "Ready, Aim, FIRE," successively, three times, each time followed by our volley in unison. Traditionally the gun salute is followed by "Taps" and from somewhere in the crowd came a recording of that lone bugel.

When the last notes faded the military honors were done, and we leaned our rifles against a fence and joined the others. My wife was there and I quietly came to stand beside her. Much of the service was in the Gwich'in language and I listened to the cluck and the hum of the preacher's voice, watched the mountains and the trees, witnessed the waning rays of the day. At the end of the reception we buried Albert Joe, first with a handful, then a shovelful at a time, and I realized he had inducted me into a band of veterans. Our connection through time and service, our individual experiences, became a collective as we executed the funeral rites. In my dissociation with the Army, my dislocation to the farthest place I could find from war, I had found an embrace only possible from one veteran to another. On that day and from then after, I wasn't just the new white teacher, I was the new veteran that banded together with the village's veterans, men that'd been there, too, in order to pay homage to a comrade.

RIDING TO STAND STILL

by Benjamin Rothman

I was just a few months out of Afghanistan and freshly into my new hobby: motorcycling. My therapist wondered why there was such an attraction to the two-wheeled vehicles amongst veterans, and particularly combat veterans. She cited anecdotal evidence of the numbers of soldiers after WWII that sparked the motorcycle culture in the southwest, noted the number of Vietnam Veterans that rode, and even looked at the uptick in sales, and accidents, of motorcycles in Iowa since our return. It had been a one year deployment for an entire brigade of the 34th Infantry Division, about 3,500 soldiers from Iowa going specifically into direct combat roles. It was also the largest deployment of soldiers from the state since World War II.

At first, I didn't really have an answer. I knew the stories as well, and I even personally knew a lot of other soldiers who had gotten motorcycles. They bought all sorts of big, noisy bikes that would literally tear up the asphalt, like Kawasaki Mean-Streaks, Harley Davidson V-Rods. Meanwhile, I had gotten an old Yamaha XV-920, a v-twin tourer from 1981; it was definitely a starter bike for me, nothing as fancy as the other guys' rides. Also by comparison, the other soldiers I knew who were getting bikes were a lot younger, in their twenties mostly, and most, if not

all, were completely unattached, whereas I was nearing forty and
happily married with two children. Our only commonality was
combat.

I chewed on that thought between therapy sessions, and actually thought about it when I rode, an almost daily occurrence that
summer. So I sat in session and told her I couldn't answer for all
riding vets, but I could at least answer for myself.

When I'm riding, there are literally only a couple of inches of
rubber between me and carnage. It requires concentration and a
hyper-attention that isn't entirely unlike being in a firefight. I am
paying attention to everything around me - the road conditions,
the other drivers, how the road curves, how my bike feels, how it
sounds, my instruments, potential hazards. Basically, I'm paying
attention to everything, a habit developed in a combat zone that
doesn't fit anywhere else in my now-civilized world.

The first time I was shot at, really shot at, time seemed to slow
down. As the adrenaline surges, everything focused so clearly that
I felt I could almost count the number of grains of sand in the air
as I took cover behind a flatbed train car wheel. Details became
crystal clear and distinct like never before only to be recalled later,
leaving me wondering "how the fuck did I track all that in such
a short time?"

I remember that the Iraqi was wearing a red Manchester United ball cap, of all things. Bright red, almost glowing it stood out
so much. In the middle of summer, 2003 we were on a Quick Reaction call to the main rail yard in Baghdad. Looters were trying
to get the contents of not only the USAID storage containers, but
anything they could carry away. We had no solid intelligence on
how many people we'd be facing or how well organized or armed
they would be. Communications with the rear were sketchy at
best, meaning that if the wind was right, our SICGARS radios
would actually be answered by our TOC, and our orders were
simply, "Do what you have to do to stop them."

One thing I noticed was that he fired his AK-47 left-handed.
His bright red hat clashed with the rest of his ensemble, which

consisted of a blue and white striped dress shirt open to the third button, dirty tan dress pants, black belt with a gold colored buckle, and black Adidas sandals over dirty feet. The sandals stood out as a little odd too, every detail of his outfit and firing stance did. Fortunately his rounds weren't accurate.

Neither was the first short burst from my machine gun, an M249 SAW. My rounds were rushed and impacted low and right. My next burst was on target, making him my first confirmed kill.

The first round took him in the abdomen, just under the ribcage and just to the right of the sternum. I saw the blood blossom almost instantly. The second bullet was higher and to my right, the way the gun pulled. It hit at about 4th rib, to the left of his sternum - definitely a lung shot but too low for a heart shot. As he was falling to the ground, the third round blasted into his left bicep above the elbow, sending his weapon into the sand with him. I could hear him moaning as best he could with one working lung and a gut wound.

We still had to secure the USAID containers and did not know how many other attackers had vanished into the railyard or how well armed they were.

Once we had passed by any wounded, we were bound by the Geneva Convention to take them into our care and protection - whether enemy or friendly and whether the enemy played by our rules or not. (We already knew they didn't.)

The jog to him seemed to take forever, but it was only fifteen shuffled steps. The heat sapped my strength and my Camelbak was already almost empty. He rolled in the sand and I saw relief in his eyes on my approach. He knew our Rules of Engagement and our own code at least as well as we did. He knew he would be safe.

I knew we had no medical resources to waste on him. We couldn't take him with us, and we couldn't afford a person to sit and guard him and reduce our numbers in any combat as we moved through hostile territory. I knew I hadn't passed him, and neither had anyone else yet. Technically, the Geneva Convention did not protect him. Not until any of us in the squad took that final step past him.

The relief on his face changed to abject terror as I raised my gun to my shoulder. My peephole sights framed his wide pain and fear filled eyes for a moment, searing itself into my memory in that instance before settling on the center of his forehead. Solidly locked on target, I gently squeezed off a single round into his skull, and stepped over his body. His red Manchester United hat lay upturned in the dirt near the pool of blood soaking into the sand, almost pristine in the afternoon sun. Voices ahead of us in the connexes caught our attention and we formed up to move further into the yard. None of us looked back.

Motorcycles invariably bring about conversation in riders, about what we ride, how we ride, and sometimes why we ride. I know that some guys, especially the younger vets, ride their motorcycles to feel alive, to remember what it felt like to be in combat.

I think I ride, mostly, to forget.

GETTING THE GOOD NEWS
by William Corley

Etched on a wooden table, the number of the Edwards A.F.B. telephone exchange waits to serve an unprepared traveler collapsing sweaty and unkempt in the reupholstered Lazy Boy implausibly sent from Muskegon to the southwest corner of the U.S.O. lounge adjacent to the PAX terminal at Bagram Air Base, Afghanistan. Clean, bright, and efficiently organized, the U.S.O. reeks of a panting desire to please, the mindless exuberance of a dog capering at dawn when its keeper comes to rebuke its barking.

A theatrical room opens from the lounge. Its square-backed couches are covered in a rough, durable fabric that resists staining from spills and effluvia. Rows are far enough apart to accommodate the legs of an average-sized man as they extend from a contorted sternum, unnaturally bent where the upper body drooped to an awkward, diagonal yearning for the seat cushion. Denied its desired destination, the head is arrested by the hard surface of a canvas-covered Kevlar helmet resting on the side of an overstuffed ALICE pack.

The movie looping on the wall is either the superhero saga du jour or a commando film composed of erotically gleeful scenes where the fitfully socialized anti-hero straps on a variety of armaments and an improbable amount of ammunition, though even ten times the amount depicted would be necessary to sustain the soundtrack of staccato blasts that lurch the film from conflict to conclusion.

Over all this waste drones the emptiness of waiting. The absence of a soldier between transports cannot be explained by comparisons to wastelands of rock and sheer precipices, nor to outer reaches of space defined more by unending cold than astronomical location. The soul is frigid, the mind supine, the senses alert and morbid, drowsy and yet longing for a reason to move.

The roar of departing flights is a mockery of escape. The only things flying today are F/A-18s "bringing the good news" to embattled Taliban caught some valleys away in a compound with someone else's women and children.

As news of successive flight cancellations spreads, those assembled disperse in shock waves of embittered expectation. The PAX terminal and U.S.O. cannot house all of the passengers accumulating like sticks against a beaver dam. Signs everywhere direct travelers waiting more than twelve hours to check-in at transient housing, a row of air-conditioned, circus-sized tents, each containing a hundred or more cots spread far enough apart to allow for the several sea-bags' worth of personal and required flotsam soldiers must carry alone through every transition from Conex box to transport home. Only the most experienced make the quarter-mile trek in which every step declares surrender.

Deafening fans blast out all thought. Day and night merge within the corona of light leaking through tent seams and door-flaps. The soul goes numb. High in the sky, the keening of Rolls Royce jet turbines reminds the ear that even objects of steel and destruction know how to mourn a people cut off before the advent of a rosy-fingered and resplendent dawn.

Note: "Getting the good news" is an idiom used to describe the delivery of ordnance during a CAS (Close-Air Support) flight.

A SOLDIER'S THANK YOU
by Allysa Kropp

'T hank you for your service," a woman said to me as she approached with her child from across the bookstore. I caught her eyes and smiled. "Thank you," doesn't seem adequate. Certainly not, "You're welcome." That would relegate it to a mere modern day pleasantry. The exchange causes me to examine the awkwardness of it, for the few seconds that it lasts. I always meet their eyes and smile warmly, caught off guard that someone noticed me in my uniform, suspended their busy day for a moment to approach me and thank me. At the post office. The coffee shop. The airport. Hardware store. Gas station. You think you don't deserve the thanks. You know you don't.

But so many do. So many have given up their youth, lost a buddy, lost a limb, missed their child's first steps, given up having a normal life, come home to an empty house, or are grappling with memories they can't process. And many have lost their lives.

There are the parents and spouses who waited in vigil, not knowing if their loved one would return. And some didn't. They deserve the recognition, and so much more from our country and each of us.

But there I am. Caught in their eye contact, smiling and

stumbling on words, and only a nod and "thank you" comes out.

What else can you say? How do you say, in those brief seconds, how grateful you are to them?

My dad served in Vietnam. He doesn't share much regarding his experience. But I have gained a sense of his pain and anger resulting from the treatment given service members when they returned home from Vietnam. He expressed concern to me one Christmas, in the middle of the U.S. wars overseas in the Middle East, for my sister returning home on R&R from Afghanistan. She would be wearing her Army uniform and traveling through Atlanta's Hartsfield airport. When I reassured him that she would travel through the airport without issue, that traveling in uniform was required until she was released on R&R, he was still unsettled. I shared with him my own experiences of traveling in uniform. I told him of the thank yous from random travelers, and the gifted cups of coffee, the occasional thanks from a flight attendant, sometimes even boarding you first. He didn't quite believe me. His memories of returning were of being surrounded by a small mob at the airport when he arrived in uniform from Vietnam. As he tried to find his duffel bags at the baggage claim, the crowd shouted verbal abuses at him. He recounted other times when he was harassed, and in one such encounter, spit on.

A few years later, I was returning home from Iraq. We refueled in Bangor, Maine on our way to Atlanta. My parents live an hour away from Bangor, and thanks to a mid-flight phone call by the kind pilot at 4 AM, they were alerted to the early Sunday morning arrival of their daughter and 274 other soldiers. I wasn't sure they would get there, as I walked down the entry hall to the lounge area with the other soldiers. My jet-lagged face disappeared into a sappy grin as I enjoyed the citizen welcome that awaited us. The Maine Troop Greeters were there to greet the flight, shaking each of our hands in a long reception line, as they have for each flight since the first Gulf War.

I know about this tradition because I grew up in Maine and went to school nearby at the University of Maine when the tradition started at the Bangor Airport in 1991. Local Mainers were proud to learn that Bangor is often the first place a service member arrives on US soil after serving for extended periods overseas. Flights with returning military frequently stop in Bangor to refuel before continuing on to their final destination. A local phone alert system began, notifying interested Mainers of each flight. The greeters offer the soldiers a small celebration on arrival, free phones, assistance, and hugs, no matter the hour. The tradition has placed Bangor, Maine in a prominent place in the hearts and memories of service members over the years. After a year or more of being in a foreign country away from your friends and family, and touching down on U.S. soil for the first time, to be the receiver of this reception is an experience without equal and lacks adequate description.

My arrival that Sunday morning was the first time my parents or I had experienced the Bangor welcome. I happily shook each hand following the line of returning soldiers, feeling odd to be receiving such appreciation at 7 AM on a Sunday morning. And then I got to the very end of the greeting party and there were my parents, shaking each of the soldiers' hands. Their handshake turned into a teary embrace when I got to them. The relief between us was palpable.

We shared a cup of coffee in the hour before my plane left for Atlanta, and I had my picture taken with the Maine Troop Greeters. It was a memorable morning, but for more reasons than I grasped that day.

It wasn't until a few months later that my Dad told me that all of the anger, pain and bitterness he had carried inside since his return from Vietnam had melted away that morning. He experienced the grass roots reception for his daughter and the plane load of soldiers, and began to heal. I realized then that that morning wasn't just my homecoming. It was his too. And for so many generations who have served before us.

So, when I awkwardly say, "Thank you," when you go out of your way to recognize my service, I am thanking you on behalf of my friends who have served, my teammates and many others who are still far away from home. I am thanking you not just for that brief moment in the book store with you, but also for the ongoing support to wounded veterans and survivor families, for the support that has lasted beyond a decade of conflict, and that now has reached back to my father's generation that didn't get a homecoming or any kind of "Thank you."

TWO SAFETY TIPS FOR THOSE RETURNING FROM DEPLOYMENTS

by Rolf Yngve

H ere's a tip: don't die.

Of course, in our profession, the ships, the sea, the battlefield all have their accidents and errors, blunders and bad luck. Your timing can be off. You can get caught up with the wrong crowd. Things happen. Sometimes fate. We know this. But, blunder and bad luck aside, there are always some people who think dying might be preferable to return.

Here's an example: coming back from deployment once, I told my pal (let's call him Dwarf) I was so depressed about my wife leaving me that I was thinking of shooting myself. As luck would have it, the tool was in hand. We were on a skeet range. Dwarf was so short he had to offset that issue by getting his bench press up to twice his weight. He stood on a box to see properly over a destroyer's bridge wing. Firearms always have an offsetting effect. Dwarf liked offsets. No wonder he liked skeet.

In naval practice, though, there is no offset for what we call a suicide ideation. Having heard me ideate suicide, Dwarf was regulation-compelled to tell my captain. The captain, then, would take me off the ship, have me examined then detached for some assignment where my potential suicide would result in no-skin-off-his-nose.

Actually, my captain would have shipped me off because he was worried about me. This guy was a particularly good man, like Dwarf, a shipmate. And when you have a shipmate like Dwarf, he doesn't tell anyone about your suicide ideation. Instead, he looks at that shotgun for shooting clay targets, and tells you, "Don't shoot yourself. Shoot her."

It had never occurred to me.

"See—you shoot yourself, you just go. Disappear. Whatever happens after that doesn't count for shit. We'll just have to find some way to fill your spot on the watch bill. You think she'll care?

I gave it some thought. I told him she might.

"So you're going to do it to make her feel bad? So she'll pay attention? That's why you want to shoot yourself? Shoot her. So you go to jail? Maybe you'll get out, maybe not, but you won't have to worry about her. You want to shoot yourself to make her feel bad? You're missing the point. Besides—if you shoot yourself, you'll make somebody have to read that teary-weary, dumb-ass letter you're going to write."

I had already written the letter.

I've always liked those letters from the combat dead, the ones that start, "Dear Mom and Dad, in case something happens..." The letters no one sees unless some blunder, bad luck or fate gets in the way.

Hoping to measure up, I bought expensive stationary, cream-colored from an expensive store. I wrote a couple of drafts, then copied a letter out by hand, measured every word. I mimicked that special courage and grace only the dead can bear, hoping if some blunder or bad luck occurred someone might read it and care about me. I wrote it to my wife, kept it in my safe to be opened and inventoried if I tried out the shotgun on my forehead. I didn't have to write a stupid, teary-weary, dumb-ass letter. It was already finished, ready, waiting to go.

"Look," Dwarf told me. "Don't shoot her. But don't shoot yourself—that's beyond dumb. Here. Shoot a clay pigeon instead. It's not all about you, asshole, you've got shipmates, too.

You've got us, and we've got you."

Here's another tip: be careful what you leave behind.

The way this works, when you don't pay the rent for your storage box, people buy up the contents and sell whatever they can. While I was away for Desert Storm, some guy got all my stuff, sold the skis, beat up furniture, old lamps, dishes, fishing gear and forgotten clothes. Then, for some reason, he looked through all the boxes of papers and bills, stories I'd written, childhood clippings my mother gave me, junk, all junk. And he found a letter.

That's why he called my dad. The storage box scavenger found his phone number in one of the pieces of mail, asked Dad if I was all right. Did I want my papers back? Dad told him he'd let me know.

The scavenger lived out in the East County portion of San Diego where the citizens and architecture are equally weathered. He had a couple of dogs, ordinary, stray-looking dogs, friendly and curious, and I found him working on an RV he told me he got after it was repossessed. Ageless sort of man in a sun bleached ball cap, whiskey voice. "I was sorry I had to sell your goods after I read that letter. Go ahead and take your papers. Here's this." He handed it to me, a cream-colored envelope bought in an expensive store, a teary-weary letter I'd written practicing to be dead. Now a stranger standing on a hardscrabble porch in the east county heat was telling me, "I thought you'd died, thought your family might have wanted it. You know, I'm glad to be able to give it to you. I'm a vet, too. Glad you're okay." He held out his hand, I shook it. He looked me carefully up and down. "How was it over there?"

I told him it was better than I had expected, not as good as I had hoped, because you're supposed to say something like that coming back from deployment. He nodded the way he was supposed to nod.

And how was that, the way he was supposed to nod? As if he understood. As if it was okay. As if I was forgiven. I had not realized I would need this forgiveness. But there it was, given.

That night, I went through those papers and got rid of bills I never paid, letters I never sent, tax forms never filed, all the stuff I had kept out of guilt or laziness, and my apartment filled with all those years when I had been happy, when I thought my wife had been happy—all the years away, all the longing, wishing, waiting sorrow for the end of one deployment or another, the movement on and on, arriving, departing, preparing to go, gone. Never there. The last four years of our marriage, we had lived with each other less than six months.

It was a Saturday night when other people were out on the town having fun, dancing, telling jokes, preening and flirting over their date-night dinners, full of hope. I hadn't thought much about my former wife for a long time. Before I shredded my teary-weary, dumb-ass letter, I read it all again feeling that stunning embarrassment over the blunders of the younger me. How could I write that sort of letter, hoping it would get printed someday? How could I hope for one of those battlefield moments, some accident of fate, error, bad timing or bad luck intervening as if somehow it would make sense out of the life I'd quit trying to carry forward? How could I have been so stupid to actually consider that shotgun?

Me living, not killed, not shot by myself or anyone else, this miserable, humiliating letter showed up and I realized, then, what the east county scavenger had forgiven. I had thought I needed to remember. My duty was to remember. It's not true. You do not have to remember the truth. We don't have to remember how we felt. We can heal. We can move on, find our own places.

Here are two tips for those of you returning from deployment: Don't die. Be careful what you leave behind.

Do that—and it won't matter the way you were; you can fix it. Do that—and you can find a way to be forgiven, and a way to forget. Do that—and there is still a chance you'll find the love you let go.

CONTRIBUTORS

Incoming's contributors in order of last name are:

SAMUEL ABEL is a California native who served overseas during Operation Iraqi Freedom as a United States Navy Hospital Corpsman. Until recently, he was living in San Diego at the ASPIRE Center, a long term residential treatment program for post-911 veterans who suffer from post traumatic stress disorder (PTSD) and traumatic brain injury (TBI) run by the Veterans Administration. He is very new to writing, enjoys it very much and hopes to continue to use literature as a creative outlet to help in his treatment and recovery.

CASONDRA BREWSTER was born in Detroit, Mich. in 1966 to a young, blue-collar couple. The oldest of four children, she was not content to stay in the Rust Belt and left home very young to travel the world. She lived in Hawaii for some time, and then ended up going to college in Wyoming. After a devastating personal loss in late 1992 she left college and joined the U.S. Army in 1993, which continued her world travels, and her writing. She served as a public affairs specialist, earning the Thomas Jefferson Military Journalist of the Year award in 2001. In 2011, after com-

pleting her B.A. in Arts and Literature, she finally left the clutch-
es of the military to pursue a full-time freelance writing career.
Within a month her first fiction short-story was published. Currently she resides in the Cascade Foothills — just a short car-ride
from Seattle — with her partner, children, a shelter-rescue dog,
and a 55-gallon aquarium of fresh-water fish. When not writing,
she tends her urban farm; you can read about her daily life on her
blog at casondrabrewster.com.

BENJAMIN BUSCH served 16 years as an infantry and light
armored reconnaissance officer in the United States Marine
Corps, deploying to Iraq in 2003 and again in 2005 where he
was wounded in the battle for Ramadi. He is the author of a
memoir, Dust to Dust, and has published in Harper's, The New
York Times Magazine, Prairie Schooner, Five Points and Michigan Quarterly Review among others. He has been a contributor
to NPR's All Things Considered and The Daily Beast. He lives
on a farm in Michigan.

SAMUEL CHAMBERLAIN is a writer, teacher, and social ac-
tivist living in Fairbanks, Alaska. He served as a combat engineer
officer and paratrooper in the Army for five years. Sam is currently pursuing an MFA in Writing at Pacific University in Oregon.

GAIL CHATFIELD is the co-founder of the Veterans Writing
Group San Diego County and author of the book, "By Dammit,
We're Marines! Veterans Stories of Heroism, Horror and Humor
in World War II on the Pacific Front."

LIAM CORLEY teaches American literature at California State
Polytechnic University, Pomona, and his work on literature and
war can be found in Chautauqua, College English, and War, Literature, and the Arts. LCDR Corley is currently on military leave
to teach at the U.S. Naval Academy in Annapolis, MD. He is a
veteran of Operation Enduring Freedom.

SIERRA CRANE was born and raised in rural Pennsylvania, homeschooled by her mother, and taught life lessons by her father. She joined the Army National Guard on her 17th birthday, ready to get out and experience the world. She served 2 tours in Iraq before her 8 years were up, discovered the Army wasn't all that she wanted, and came home to realize she never really gave much thought to what she wanted to do for the rest of my life if it wasn't the military. Writing was a great way to escape those feelings of loss and regret after her enlistment was up. Now back in her hometown, she is serving in a different way, as a police officer, and thinks she's finally found where she belongs.

DOUG D'ELIA was born in Massachusetts and served as a medic during the Vietnam War (1964-1969). He is a member of the Syracuse Veterans Writer's Group, and the author of four books. A complete list of his work can be viewed at dougdelia.com.

JULIA DIXON EVANS is a writer in San Diego. Her short fiction can be found in Hobart, Monkeybicycle, Noble/Gas Qtrly, Swarm, Broad!, Black Candies, and elsewhere. Her short story, "Nineteen Things Only People Who Are Not Going To Survive The Hour Will Understand" was nominated for the 2015 Best of the Net. Her short story, "Fiddle De Dee" was long-listed for Ellen Datlow's "Best of Horror" in 2013. She was a recipient of a PEN in the Community Residency in 2014 and a Poets & Writers Grant in 2015 for teaching and facilitating writing workshops.

ALEX FLYNN is a photojournalist currently splitting his time between New York City and Missouri. He enlisted in the United States Army in 2008 and spent four years as a infantryman, then three more as a combat correspondent. Other than a brief stint in Japan, the Army didn't show him much other than Afghanistan. He is currently working on projects as a full time freelance photojournalist. He hopes to continue to use his written and photographic work to contribute to the narrative of the veteran experience.

C. S. GRIFFIN'S promising 11 year military career was cut short after a deployment to Iraq. He now teaches at a juvenile detention center in Rapid City, SD, where he lives with his wife and children. Mr. Griffin has enjoyed being published many times in the past, but spends most of his free time with his family these days. He still plans on writing the great American novel one day.

KELLI HEWLETT is a Registered Nurse finishing her Bachelor's degree in nursing at San Diego State University. She was born into a military family at Fort Jackson, South Carolina, where she started her own army career 18 years later. She got her start in health care as a Licensed Practical Nurse and fell in love with the profession and efforts to assist the public. For her work in aiding the community she has received a Certificate of Recognition from California State Senator Joel Anderson.

JUSTIN HUDNALL serves as the Executive Director of So Say We All, a San Diego-based 501c3 literary arts organization, and is an Independent Producer with KPBS for the veteran writer radio showcase, "Incoming." His prior career was in international emergency aide with the United Nations in New York and South Sudan. He graduated from NYU's Tisch School of the Arts with a BFA in playwriting, is a San Diego Foundation Creative Catalyst Fellow, and a PEN USA Teaching Fellow.

KURT KALBFLEISCH is a writer who still works for the US Navy to pay the bills. He joined the US Navy after graduating from high school in 1979. Following his training as a Fire Controlman, Kurt's first two assignments were as a Close-In Weapon System technician aboard USS JOHN F KENNEDY (CV 67) and USS SAVANNAH (AOR 4). After serving as part of the commissioning crew of USS GARY (FFG 51), Kurt served as a Close-In Weapon System instructor at Service School Command, Great Lakes, Illinois. After his initiation as a Chief Petty Officer, Kurt joined the commissioning crew of USS COWPENS (CG 63), where he served as Leading Chief Petty Officer of the combined Gunnery and Cruise Missile divisions. On 17 January 1993, the 212th anniversary of the Revolutionary War battle for which his ship was named, Kurt led the crew in a Tomahawk missile strike against targets in Iraq. Following a tour as an instructor at Fleet Combat Training Center, Pacific in San Diego, Kurt returned to sea in USS ELLIOT (DD 967) as Leading Chief of Strike Warfare division. He retired from the Navy in 2002, and now lives with his family in La Mesa, California.

BROOKE KING served in the United States Army, deploying to Iraq in 2006 as a wheel vehicle mechanic, machine gunner, and recovery specialist. As a wife to a fellow veteran and mother to twin boys who were conceived in Iraq, Brooke began writing her unique experience down as a way to cope with PTSD, but found that her writing ability along with her combat experience gave her a distinct voice within the war genre. Since obtaining her Bachelors from Saint Leo University, Brooke has refocused her writing, bringing perspective and insight into the involvement of female soldiers in combat and war. Her work has been published in the, O-Dark-Thirty, War Literature and the Arts, Press 53's fiction war anthology Home of the Brave: Somewhere in the Sand, University of Nebraska Press and Potomac's "Red, White, and True" Anthology, as well as Prairie Schooner's Winter 2013 Literary Magazine. Her chapbook, "Love in the Shape of a War Zone," was released in October 2013 by Green Rabbit Press. Currently, Brooke is working on her memoir, Inscriptions From a Time When at War.

LT. COL. ALLYSA KROPP lives in Alexandria, VA and has served in the Virginia Army National Guard since 1995. She has deployed to Guatemala, Bosnia and Iraq. Her parents Marcia and Ted Kropp encouraged military service in their ten children. Her father served as a Naval Intelligence Officer, which included intelligence operations in Vietnam. He retired as a Captain in the US Navy Reserves in the late 1980s. Her father's service inspired Allysa's career as well as inspired her brother's service as a US Marine, and the military service of two sisters, one as a pilot who later retired from the US Army Reserves, and one who served in the Regular Army as a transportation officer, deploying to Afghanistan and Iraq. Allysa is thankful for her father's service and mentorship, and for the generations of veterans that served before her.

BRANDON LINGLE'S work appears widely in places like The New York Times, TIME, The North American Review, Guernica, Epiphany, Slate.com, National Geographic.com, Narrative, War, Literature & the Arts, Evergreen Review, and Mississippi Review. His essays are notables in The Best American Essays 2010 and 2013. Raised in Southern California, Brandon is an active-duty Air Force officer who's served in Iraq and Afghanistan, taught in the English Department at the U.S. Air Force Academy, and currently lives in Northern California. He serves as Art Director and Nonfiction Editor of War, Literature & the Arts: An International Journal of the Humanities.

NATALIE LOVEJOY is composer, lyricist, and bookwriter whose work has been heard at 54 Below, The Duplex, Laurie Beechman Theatre, The Flea Theatre, Greenwhich Music House, and in Nashville at the legendary Bluebird Café, and she is listed in The Directory of Contemporary Musical Theatre Writers at www.comtemporarymusicaltheatre.com. Her original musical Deployed, which she began writing while married to a soldier deployed to Iraq, premiered off-off Broadway at the Abingdon Theatre Company in November 2013 and played again at the Gene Frankel Theatre in January 2014 to sold-out audiences. Her education includes NYU Steinhardt (MM in Music Composition), Catholic University (BM in Musical Theater), the BMI Lehman Engel Musical Theatre Workshop, and the Johnny Mercer Musical Theatre Project at Northwestern University. She is a

Professional Member of ASCAP and The Dramatist Guild. www.
natalielovejoy.nyc

TENELY LOZANO graduated from the United States Coast
Guard Academy in 2008, then was commissioned as an officer
in the US Coast Guard. During her five years as an officer, she
was stationed on a ship and then attended Navy Dive School and
spent two years as a diver. She is currently working on an MFA
in Creative Nonfiction Literature from Sierra Nevada College.

ANDREW HANSEN MILLER served in the U.S. Army from
2006 to 2012, Afghanistan, twice, and picked up the pen (again)
in Syracuse, New York after becoming inspired by his beloved
mentors and fellow veterans in the Syracuse Veterans Writing
Group and Syracuse University. He writes because nothing lasts
forever, but writing comes close. He claims close friends & family
from Barrington, Illinois; Charlotte, North Carolina; Syracuse,
New York; the 101st Airborne Division; the 10th Mountain Division; and Illinois Wesleyan University. He loves the beach, sing-
ing, painting, Plutobear the cat, skiing, the smell of pine trees,
and, most of all, Delmore Schwartz's poem Calmly We Walk
through This April's Day. He misses his father.

ANTHONY MOLL is a recently repatriated Californian. His
work has appeared in O-Dark-Thirty, Gertrude Journal and Assar-
acus, and he writes about books for Baltimore's Gay Life magazine.
He holds an MFA in creative nonfiction and is pursuing a PhD in
writing and literature at University of California, Santa Cruz.

LISBETH PRIFOGLE served her country as a United States
Marine officer, and is currently working on a memoir about her
experiences in a war zone. Lisbeth holds an MFA from Antioch
University - Los Angeles. Her work was featured in Poem Mem-
oir Story, The Splinter Generation, Citron Review, and In the
Know Travel. Lisbeth is an active member of the Bayou Writers

Club where she gives presentations and writes articles about the craft and business of writing. She lives in Louisiana.

BENJAMIN ROTHMAN – Ben unless he's in trouble – retired in 2014 from 23 years of combined service in the active duty Army, Army Reserves and National Guard. Courtesy of the military he has travelled much of the world and gone sightseeing by gun sight in some of the best vacation spots: South Korea in 1997; Iraq in 2003; Kosovo in 2007; and Afghanistan in 2010. In that time he served as a Cavalry Scout, a Chemical Warfare Defense Specialist, and his favorite position, a Combat Medic. Rothman quite happily transitioned to civilian life and is enjoying his new career working for the University of Iowa doing IT support. He lives in rural Iowa with his wife Sarah, their children Spenser and Molly, two dogs, a cat, cockatiel, and three chickens. All of which on occasion make life in a combat zone seem make much more appealing than it really was.

JIM RULAND is a veteran of the U.S. Navy and the author of Forest of Fortune, the short story collection Big Lonesome, and co-author with Scott Campbell Jr. of Discovery Channel's Deadliest Catch of Giving the Finger, and with Keith Morris on his punk rock memoir My Damage (forthcoming 2016). His work has received awards from Bread Loaf, Canteen, Reader's Digest, San Diego Book Awards and the National Endowment for the Arts. He is the books columnist for San Diego CityBeat and a contributor to the Los Angeles Times. His fiction and nonfiction have appeared in The Believer, Electric Literature, Esquire, Granta, Hobart, Oxford American Magazine and more. Ruland has taught writing at Northern Arizona University, Santa Monica College and at San Diego Writers, Ink and has served as a visiting writer/guest lecturer at Cal State Channel Islands, Oklahoma University, University of California Riverside Palm Desert Low Residency, PEN in the Community, Radford University, and Santa Fe University of Art and Design.

ROBERT SHAW is a Bronze Star decorated U.S. Army Veteran. He served as a Captain in 1/8 Infantry Battalion, 4th ID during OIF I. F. He is a published photographer, advanced SCUBA diver, licensed general contractor, ordained minister, entrepreneur, and proud husband and father.

G. MICHAEL SMITH served four years as a Navy diesel mechanic (EN3) between 1967 and 1971. Home-ported out of Long Beach Naval Station on ocean-going mine sweepers (MSO's,) he did three Western Pacific (WESPAC) tours with the Iron Men in Wooden Ships. His MSOs were part of Operation Market Time and Operation End Sweep, doing ICORPS coastal patrol board-and-search and mine sweeping operations near and at the DMZ in Vietnam. Between tours, Smith served as a Shore Patrolman out of Los Angeles International Airport's military police office, conducting foot patrols and enforcement at LAX and military arrests in the surrounding communities in cooperation with LAPD.

MARIAH SMITH is an active duty military police officer currently assigned to Fort Bragg as the XO for a Criminal Investigation Battalion. She grew up in a Navy family but never liked the water, so she decided to join the Army and jump out of airplanes. She has deployed six times in support of the War on Terror including tours as a platoon leader and company commander. She is most proud of leading a platoon in the initial invasion into Iraq in 2003. Her most recent three deployments have all been in Afghanistan, a place she has come to love but not quite understand. Her other assignments have included serving as a Congressional Fellow for Congressman Steve Israel, an Inspector General for HQDA, and as Education Director for the CSA's Soldier for Life office. She is a graduate of Vanderbilt University and the FBI National Academy, session 256. When she is not deployed she enjoys riding horses, hanging out with the pets, and spending all her deployment money to fix up old houses (currently on #3). In the evenings she tries to write while limiting herself to one glass of bourbon. She is not always successful.

GILL SOTU isn't strictly a poet, a musician, a writer, a DJ or host, but strives to combine the artistic elements of himself as he strives to be an ever present forceful undercurrent of soulful, comedic, thought-provoking passion that engages and inspires his audiences throughout California. Gill is currently the host of Neo Soul Tuesday at the Onyx Room, Raw Artist Showcase at the House Of Blues, Train Of Thought Podcast & Radio Show on KNSJ 89.1, as well as being selected to be the first Artist in Residence for the Jacob's Center For Neighborhood Innovation.

ADAM STONE is a retired Marine Corps Gunnery Sergeant with 20 years of service including multiple combat tours in the middle east. He is married with four kids, and at the time of writing his piece, a freshman at San Diego City College.

ERIC STRAND is currently a medical student at The University of North Carolina at Chapel Hill. He was an enlisted service member in the army for 14 years, where he served in Army Special Forces. He had 3 combat tours to Iraq between 2004 and 2008, and was medically discharged for a service connected cancer in 2013.

ANDREW SZALA separated from the Army in May after eight years. He served as a Combat Medic and Licensed Practical Nurse, and saw combat in Afghanistan in 2009/2010. In the past year, he's lost four friends to suicide and PTSD-related issues, in addition to witnessing firsthand many of the issues today's veterans face. He appreciates that someone is taking the time to actually let veterans' voices be heard.

VANCE VOYLES spent seven and a half years in the U.S. Army

working as an Arabic Linguist overseas and stateside. After attending college, he transitioned into law enforcement where he spent the last thirteen years, seven of which were spent working as a Sex Crimes and Homicide detective in central Florida. While doing so, he also received his MFA in creative writing at the University of Central Florida. His work is included in Creative Nonfiction's anthology--True Crime: Real-life stories of grave-robbing, identity theft, abduction, addiction, obsession, murder, and more. Other selections of his work have been featured in Burrow Press Review, J Journal, Rattle Magazine, O-Dark-Thirty, Hippocampus, and Pithead Chapel Review. He is currently working on a memoir, Waiving Miranda: Confessions of a Sex Crimes Detective, about his time in law enforcement and maintains a blog at www.waivingmiranda.com.

NATHAN S. WEBSTER reported several times from Iraq as a freelance photojournalist, and his work appeared in newspapers across the country. Recent work has appeared in The New York Times, the Daily Beast and other venues. He is also an Army veteran of Desert Storm.

BRENT WINGFIELD is a former U.S. Army Sergeant with combat experience in Iraq and Afghanistan. He has always enjoyed writing, primarily as a means of coping, and he now spends his time pontificating about the eight years he spent in the Infantry. His favorite writers are Hemingway and Kafka. Brent enjoys long walks on the beach, craft beer, and belt-fed machine-guns.

DERRICK WOODFORD'S current job with the federal government inspired his move to the San Diego area over ten years ago. When not working, Derrick pursues his interest in creative writing and filmmaking. He holds a MFA in Creative Writing and a Certificate of Completion from UCSD Extension in Video Production.

ROLF YNGVE rose from seaman to captain during a thirty-five year active-duty career in the US Navy. A surface warfare officer, he commanded a destroyer, served as the US Defense Attaché to Rome, and deployed for naval operations at sea with eleven different ships and staffs. Rolf holds an MFA from Warren Wilson, was a 2012 MacDowell Colony Fellow, and a 2014 Bread Loaf Camargo Residency Fellow. He is the fiction editor for Shadowgraph Magazine and teaches resume writing to veterans in recovery at Veterans Village of San Diego. He lives in Coronado, California, with his spouse, Sharon Shelton, Captain, USN (retired).

MATT YOUNG is a veteran, writer, and teacher. His work can be found or is forthcoming in BULL, Midwestern Gothic, and O-Dark-Thirty. He's currently pursuing an MA in creative writing at Miami University, in Oxford, Ohio.

Addendum:

Thank you so much for reading Incoming. It means a lot to both of us at So Say We All and the contributors in this collection. We'd love to hear from you about what you thought of it: comments, questions, maybe you've got a story yourself you'd like to share or know someone who does. Whatever you have to say, we'd like to hear it at info@sosayweallonline.com, or you can reach Executive Director Justin Hudnall at justinhudnall@sosayweallonline.com.

Best,

So Say We All
(Justin and Julia)

SO SAY WE ALL

.